*Law*Basics

SCOTTISH LEGAL SYSTEM

SECOND EDITION

AUSTRALIA
Law Book Co.
Sydney

CANADA and USA
Carswell
Toronto

HONG KONG
Sweet & Maxwell Asia

NEW ZEALAND
Brookers
Wellington

SINGAPORE and MALAYSIA
Sweet & Maxwell Asia
Singapore and Kuala Lumpur

*Law*Basics

SCOTTISH LEGAL SYSTEM

SECOND EDITION

By

Robert S. Shiels, M.A., LL.B., LL.M., Ph.D.

Solicitor in the Supreme Courts of Scotland

THOMSON
™
W. GREEN

Published in 2003 by

W. Green & Son Ltd
21 Alva Street
Edinburgh EH2 4PS

www.wgreen.co.uk

Reprinted 2006, 2008

Printed and bound in Great Britain by
TJ International Ltd, Padstow, Cornwall

No natural forests were destroyed to make this product;
Only farmed timber was used and replanted

A CIP catalogue record for this book is available from the British Library

ISBN 13: 978-0-414-01551-7

CONTENTS

Page

Table of Cases vii

1. The Development of Scots Law 1
2. The Sources of Scots Law 8
3. Courts and Tribunals 13
4. The Personnel 27
5. Legislation and Precedent....................................... 39
6. Civil Litigation 53
7. Criminal Justice 60
8. The Future 68

Appendix 1. Glossary and Latin Maxims and Phrases 72
Appendix 2. Analysis of a Case 76
Appendix 3. Technique for Answering Exam Questions.................. 78
Appendix 4. Sample Examination Questions and Answer Plans...... 80

Index 83

TABLE OF CASES

Page

ADAM V MCNEILL, 1971 S.L.T. (Notes) 80 65
Advocate, H.M. v Milford, 1973 S.L.T. 12 63
Anderson v H.M. Advocate, 1974 S.L.T. 239 68
Anderson v H.M. Advocate, 1996 S.L.T. 155 .... 12, 31, 52
Annandale and Hartfell (Earldom of) [1986] A.C. 319 14
Arenson v Casson Beckman Rutley & Co. [1975] 3 All E.R. 901 14

BANNATYNE V LORD OVERTOUN (1904) 7 F. (H.L.) 1 14
Bartonhill Coal Co. v Reid (1858) 3 Macq. 266 6
Batchelor v Pattison and Mackersy (1876) 3 R. 914 31
Bell v Ogilvie (1863) 2 M. 336 32
Black v Glasgow Corporation, 1958 S.C. 260 49
Black v H.M. Advocate, 1991 S.C.C.R. 1 68
Blair v Assets Co. (1896) 23 R. (H.L.) 36 33
Boosma v Clark and Rose Ltd, 1983 S.L.T. (Sh.Ct.) 67 52
Botterills of Blantyre v Hamilton District Licensing Board, 1986 S.L.T. 14 21
Brennan v H.M. Advocate, 1977 J.C. 38 52
British Steamship Co. v Lithgows Ltd, 1975 S.C. 110 58
Brown v Hamilton D.C., 1983 S.L.T. 397 22
Brown v Stott, 2001 S.L.T. 59 23
Bruce v Smith (1890) 17 R. 1000 11
Buchanan v Davidson (1877) 14 S.L.R. 233 32
Burmah Oil Co. Ltd v Lord Advocate, 1964 S.C. (H.L.) 49
Burns v H.M. Advocate, 1995 S.L.T. 1090 11

CAMPBELL AND COSANS V UK (1982) 4 E.H.R.R. 293 12
Commercial Union Assurance v Waddell, 1919 S.C. (H.L.) 38 14
Commerzbank AG v Large, 1977 S.C. 375 51
Cooper v Cooper (1888) 15 R. (H.L.) 21 .... 14, 51
Copeland v H.M. Advocate, 1987 S.C.C.R. 232 .... 25, 52
Caven v Cumming, 1998 S.L.T. 768 61

DA COSTA EN SCHAAKE NV V NEDERLANDSE BELASTINGADMINISTRATIE
    [1963] C.M.L.R. 224 51
Dalgleish v Glasgow Corporation, 1976 S.C. 32 52
Dana v Stevenson, 1989 S.L.T. (Sh.Ct) 43 34
Defrenne v Sabena {1976] 2 C.M.L.R. 98 42
Dekker, 2000 S.C.L.R. 1087 22
Dixon v Rutherford (1863) 2 M. 61 32
Donnelly v Donnelly, 1959 S.C. 97 52
Donoghue v Stevenson, 1932 S.C. (H.L.) 31 80

Drew v Drew (1870) 9 M. 163 10
Dumfries C.C. v Phyn (1895) 22 R. 538 61

ELLIOTT V JOICEY, 1935 S.C. (H.L.) 57 .... 14, 51
Equity and Law Life Assurance Society v Tritonia Ltd, 1943 S.C. (H.L.) 58 34

FARRELL V FARRELL, 1990 S.C.L.R. 717 52
Ferguson v Maclennan Salmon Co., 1990 S.L.T. 658 15

GARLAND V B.R. ENGINEERING LTD [1982] 2 C.M.L.R. 174 .... 43, 81
Glasgow Corporation v Central Land Board, 1956 S.C. (H.L.) 1 79
Gordon v Kirkcaldy D.C., 1990 S.L.T. 644 48
Gordon v Nakeski Cumming, 1924 S.C. 939 34
Grant v Sun Shipping Co. Ltd, 1948 S.C. (H.L.) 73 14
Greenshields v Magistrates of Edinburgh (1710–1711) Rob. 12 5
Grieve v Edinburgh and District Water Trs, 1918 S.C. 700 10

HAMILTON V EMSLIE (1868) 7 M. 173 33
Hay v H.M. Advocate, 1968 J.C. 40 63
Herron v Nelson, 1976 S.L.T. (Sh.Ct.) 42 52
Hunter v Glasgow Corporation, 1971 S.C. 220 52
Inland Revenue Commissioners v Luke, 1963 S.C. (H.L.) 65 48

INTERNATIONALE HANDELSGESELLSCHAFT MBH V EINFUHR- UND VORRATSSTELLE
    FUR GETREIDE UND FUTTERMITTEL (11/70) [1970] E.C.R. 1125 12
Islip Pedigree Breeding Centre v Abercromby, 1959 S.L.T. 161 58

JESSOP V STEVENSON, 1988 S.L.T. 223 52

KAUR V LORD ADVOCATE, 1981 S.L.T. 322 12
Kaye v Hunter, 1958 S.C. 208 22
Kennedy v Spratt [1972] A.C. 99 14
Kirkwood v H.M. Advocate, 1939 J.C. 36 52
Kostric v O'Hara, 1990 S.C.L.R. 129 19
Kruse v Johnson [1998] 2 Q.B. 91 47

LEADBETTER V HUTCHESON, 1934 J.C. 70 48
Lee v H.M. Advocate, 1968 S.L.T. 155 28
Lord Advocate's Reference No.1 of 2001, 2002 S.L.T. 466 50
Lothian R.C. v T, 1984 S.L.T. (Sh.Ct.) 74 52
Lugano v Ayrshire Valuation Appeal Committee, 1972 S.C. 314 20

MACBETH AND MACLAGAN V MACMILLAN, 1914 S.C. (J.) 165 34
McCann v Anderson, 1981 S.L.T. (Lands Tr.) 13 11
MacDonald of Keppoch, Petr, 1989 S.L.T. (Lyon Ct.) 2 19
McIntosh v British Railways Board, 1990 S.L.T. 641 15
Macintosh v Lord Advocate (1876) 3 R. (H.L.) 34 22
Mackintosh v Fraser (1860) 22 D. 421 31
Macleod v Levitt, 1969 J.C. 16 68
Macmillan v McConnell, 1917 J.C. 43 47
McPhelin v H.M. Advocate, 1960 J.C. 17 65
McPherson v Boyd, 1907 S.C. (J.) 43 27
Marshall v Scottish Milk Marketing Board, 1956 S.C. (H.L.) 37 52
Martinez v Grampian Health Board, 1996 S.L.T. 69 .... 15, 59
Meechan v McFarlane, 1996 S.L.T. 208 58
Moore v Secretary of State, 1985 S.L.T. 38 12
Moran v H.M. Advocate, 1990 S.C.C.R. 40 64
Morgan Guaranty Trust Co v Lothian R.C., 1995 S.L.T. 299 11

Munro's Trs v Munro, 1971 S.C. 280........ 52

NOLD V E.G. COMMISSION [1974] E.C.R. 419........ 12

OLIVER V SADDLER, 1929 S.C. (H.L.) 94........ 51
Orr Ewing's Trs v Orr Ewing (1885) 13 R. (H.L.) 1........ 51
Outram v Lees, 1992 S.L.T. 32........ 67

PEPPER V HART [1993] A.C. 593........ 49

R V HENDRY, 1955 S.L.T. (Notes) 66........ 22
R. v Secretary of State for Transport, *ex p*. Factortame (No. 2) [1990] C.M.L.R. 217........ 42
R. (Majead) v Immigration Appeal Tribunal (2003) 147 S.J.L.B. 539........ 77
Renfrewshire Assessor v Hendry, 1969 S.C. 211........ 48
Ritchie v Pirie, 1972 J.C. 7........ 52
Robbie The Pict v H.M. Advocate, 2002 S.C.C.R. 213........ 34
Royal Four Towns Fishing Association v Dumfriesshire Assessor, 1956 S.L.T. 217........ 11

SANDERSON V CAMPBELL (1833) 11 S. 623........ 32
Scott v Aberdeen Corporation, 1976 S.C. 81........ 49
Scottish Discount Co v Blin, 1986 S.L.T. 123........ 52
Shillingday v Smith, 1998 S.L.T. 976........ 11
Short's Trs v Keeper of the Registers of Scotland, 1994 S.L.T. 65........ 49
Slater v H.M. Advocate, 1928 J.C. 94........ 23
Spencer v Spencer, 1983 S.L.T. (Sh.Ct.) 87........ 52
Steward v Mclean, Baird and Neilson, 1915 S.C. 13........ 33
Stock v Jones [1978] 1 All E.R. 948........ 48
Strathclyde R.C. v Sheriff Clerk (Glasgow), 1992 S.L.T. (Sh.Ct.) 79........ 34
Strathern v Padden, 1926 J.C. 9........ 48
Swinfern v Lord Chelmsford (1860) 5 H.& N. 890........ 31

T V SECRETARY OF STATE FOR SCOTLAND, 1987 S.C.C.R. 65........ 22
Templeton v E, 1998 S.C.L.R. 672........ 34
Thomas v Thomas, 1947 S.C. (H.L.) 45........ 15
Thoms v Bain (1888) 15 R. 613........ 32
Tudhope v McKee, 1987 S.C.C.R. 663........ 50

VAN GEND EN LOOS [1963] C.M.L.R. 105........ 42

WALKINGSHAW V MARSHALL, 1992 S.C.C.R. 1167........ 43, 81
Wan Ping Nam v German Minister of Justice, 1972 J.C. 43........ 68
Westwater v Thomson, 1992 S.C.C.R. 624........ 43, 81
Wilson v Hill, 1943 J.C. 124........ 66

X V SWEENEY, 1982 J.C. 70........ 61
X Insurance Co v A and B, 1936 S.C. 225........ 33

"A legal system is a coercive order of public rules addressed to rational persons for the reasons of regulating their conduct and providing the framework for social co-operation. When these rules are just they establish a basis for legitimate expectations. They constitute grounds upon which persons can rely on one another and rightly object when their expectations are not fulfilled. If the bases of these claims are unsure, so are the boundaries of man's liberties."

John Rawls, *A Theory of Justice* (1971)

1. THE DEVELOPMENT OF SCOTS LAW

INTRODUCTION

The work of jurists can be divided into various distinctive areas, each depending on the specific subject matter under consideration. Analytical jurisprudence, for example, involves the scientific analysis of legal structures and concepts and the empirical exercise of discerning and elucidating the basic elements constituting law in specific legal systems. Historical jurisprudence, by way of contrast, is a study of the historical development and growth of legal systems and the changes involved in that growth. There are, of course, other distinct areas reflecting differing perspectives, including, but not limited to, sociological and economic jurisprudence.

These distinctions are mentioned at the outset because the study of a legal system involves the rational or orderly inquiry into the legal structures of a particular political area or country. In doing so, the historical development of that country must be considered because the growth of law is so closely bound up with political, social and economic growth and change. Moreover, the nature of a society in which early developments took place can be crucial in determining the later structures.

This book is concerned with reviewing, too briefly it must be admitted, the broader elements constituting the legal system of that part of the United Kingdom known as Scotland. The Scottish legal system is considered on its own for this is not a comparative study, comparing and contrasting our system with another. It seems clear, moreover, writing early in 2003, that in three or four years' time the description of the Scottish legal system will be different, particularly as major public law initiatives result in changes to government in its broadest sense.

The present Scottish legal system, and the complex body of doctrines, principles and rules which are to be found within that system, did not flow from a single Act of Parliament. It represents a long, slow and spasmodic process of evolution. The influences brought to bear vary with peace and war and related politics. The development of the Scottish legal system is in truth an historical process and to that extent a consideration of some Scottish history is necessary to see how things came to pass.

THE FEUDAL PERIOD

With the victory of Carham over the Northumbrians in 1018, the Kingdom of Scotland attained its present boundaries. The arrival of the Normans, however, pacified England in and after 1066 and began in Scotland about 1080. An important factor was the marriage of Malcolm III to the Saxon Princess Margaret about 1070, for she brought Anglo-

Saxon influences to bear on Scottish institutions. The marriage of their sons Alexander I and David I to English noblewomen continued that process. The process of Anglicisation or Anglo-Normanisation was definite from the reign of David I (1124–1153). Prior to these developments the law was probably entirely customary. Slowly the custom came to be embodied with written law, especially in charters. It was in this era that the system of feudal tenure developed. This was because the Scottish kings followed the Norman practice of conferring land upon incomers and in return the kings received the loyalty of the recipients and the promise of armed men in war. The tenants would create their own sub-tenants and so on down, until the peasants who were given land returned produce or labour.

The government that resulted from this form of reciprocal loyalty brought about a centralised system with ultimately all rights derived from the Crown. The Royal Chancery issued the charters conferring the lands or confirming them. Disputes about these matters resulted in investigations following an issue of a legal unit called a brieve.

Over time the burghs developed and, with different social and material considerations there from rural areas, the feudal system was looser. Feudalism changed because the constant dispersal of power from tenant to sub-tenant meant that support for the sovereign or his successor became less direct and dependable.

Arguably, the feudal system gave a certain cohesion to Scottish society in emphasising the loyalty owed by everyone in Scotland to the person of the king, both personally and as a symbol of the nation. The system encouraged the growth of courts and, at the centre, the *curia regis* or royal court gave counsel to the king. In time that gathering developed into the Privy Council. There were class divisions in feudalism but as they developed so too did the idea of a national constitution.

THE LATER MIDDLE AGES

The early period of legal development was ended abruptly by the death of Alexander III in 1286 and by the death also of the heiress to the throne, the Maid of Norway in 1290. In 1291 Edward I of England attempted to incorporate Scotland into England, which provoked the War of Independence. The period from Bannockburn in 1329 to the Union of the Crowns in 1603 was a period of political dispute and economic troubles. The feudal pattern began to dissolve and after the first Parliament at Cambuskenneth meetings were more frequent. The representatives of the burghs attended more regularly, especially from 1357 as their agreement was thought necessary for the levying of taxes.

From the mid-fourteenth century the presence of these burgesses was normal at Parliament, the supreme court of law. There, following French practice, Parliament came to be referred to as the Assembly of the Three Estates, or the Estates. These were the clergy, tenants-in-chief and burgesses, although this varied over time. The Three Estates met separately for deliberating and discussion as well as jointly in a single chamber. The delegation of parliamentary powers to committees resulted in a Committee for Causes, and from all that and similar judicial committees there developed the Court of Session.

Influences on the development of the law in Scotland varied over the course of this long period. The canon law of the Church may have affected the law prior to the Reformation but thereafter it declined. Similarly Roman law was less referred to and over time it died away also. Further, sources such as the *Regiam Majestatem* and *Quonian Attachiamenta* described law and practice in the earliest periods. These texts were relied on in later centuries but their importance diminished with changed conditions. Finally, there was a tendency of Scots students of law to attend French and later Dutch universities, and their education there introduced them to developments that were substantially different to those in England.

In this brief survey mention must be made of the reign of two monarchs in particular. Under James IV (1488–1513) the administration of justice improved with the king personally taking an active part in the justice-ayres (or circuit courts) all over the kingdom. Moreover, under James V (1513–1542) a number of notable developments were headed by the foundation of the College of Justice. This was authorised in 1535 by papal bull and in 1541 the Scottish Parliament confirmed the first institution of the college in 1532, ratified the bull and ordained that the college should remain perpetually for the administration of justice in the kingdom. The senators of the college were given powers to make Acts for the ordering of process and the expedition of justice, which became Acts of Sederunt. The coherence brought to the law by these changes cannot be overstated.

Papal authority was eroded by alternative ideas of civil and religious government. The Scots followed the Calvinistic idea of two kingdoms, one civil and the other spiritual. These two jurisdictions were complementary. When the Estates met in 1560, John Knox's Confession of Faith was ratified and the papal authority abolished, mass forbidden and the previous religious practices condemned. An Act in 1560 abolished all papal jurisdictions and brought to an end the religious courts and appeals to Rome.

In 1563 the establishment of a Commissary Court in Edinburgh with four judges allowed matters previously dealt with by the old church courts, such as marriage, divorce and legitimacy, to be dealt with there for the whole of Scotland. The subsequent development of judicial divorce represented a major change indicating the reduction of previous ideas.

THE UNION OF THE CROWNS

The only child of Queen Mary of Scotland, James VI, was also heir to the English throne and he inherited that on the death of Queen Elizabeth.

James VI and I took a close interest in the government of his two kingdoms and the result was a period of comparative stability.

The constant theme of this period was the closer political union which James worked for on the principle that two realms with one king should be treated as one. Projects and literature for closer union expanded, but little practical changes were brought about. The exception was the institution in 1617 of the General Register of Sasines, which maintained a continuous record of all transactions relating to or affecting landed property. The validity and security of these transactions was enhanced with the introduction in 1672 of a minute-book recording those in whose favour charters and writs were given. James was able to have repealed certain English statutes which treated Scotland as a hostile country. In Calvin's Case (1608) it was held that Scots born after the accession of James VI to the English throne were not aliens in England. Similar provision was made by the Scottish Parliament for the king's English subjects.

The seventeenth century was dominated by a long series of disputes about religion, and the role of the monarch, and this took precedence over nationhood. The reigns of Charles I and Charles II were notable for the political and religious struggles which affected legal developments. This was especially so given the autocratic nature of government: the use by Charles II of the Scottish Privy Council to rule Scotland led to the Council exercising both legislative and judicial functions, thus challenging Parliament and the Court of Session respectively. The royal prerogative, the residual powers of the king as the fountain of justice, was the purported authority for such action.

The elements of constitutional law were only too apparent in the civil war and religious antagonism of the seventeenth century. And yet, despite the political turmoil, private law was greatly developed and improved. Influential changes were made to the law in this period, *e.g.* prescription, by the Prescription Acts of 1617 and 1699, and the execution of deeds, by the Subscription of Deeds Act 1681.

The period is notable also for the influence of major jurists. Sir Thomas Craig of Riccarton (1540–1607) produced his work *Jus Feudale* in 1603 and it became the first institutional text, but there were other eminent writers of the age, the greatest of whom was Lord Stair (1619–1695). His work *Institutions* was published in 1681, and revised and enlarged for a second edition in 1693, and this marked the creation of modern Scots law.

THE EIGHTEENTH CENTURY

In 1689 there was a further attempt to achieve a union of Parliaments. Commissioners were again appointed but nothing was achieved. In 1700 further tentative moves were made to discuss union but English reluctance blocked progress. The death of Queen Anne's children added the element of concern for the succession and a possible source of friction between England and Scotland. The antagonism between the two countries suggested complete separation and that was accentuated by provocative legislation from each Parliament.

However, in 1706 Queen Anne nominated Commissioners and thus began the process again. Earlier drafts of a treaty from previous meetings allowed swift progress. The articles of union were debated and approved with minor amendments by the Scottish Parliament on January 16, 1707. Similar legislation was passed by the English Parliament. The Scottish Privy Council, by a proclamation, dissolved the Scottish Parliament on April 28, 1707. On May 1, 1707, the United Kingdom of Great Britain came into being. The English Parliament was not dissolved but the members simply became members of the Parliament of Great Britain and the procedure remained the same.

The immediate aftermath of the Union was unsettled, with several events suggesting strongly to the Scots that the Treaty was being breached by the English to the latter's advantage. English law of treason was imposed in Scotland in 1708.

In 1711 the Duke of Hamilton and Brandon had a British title conferred on him but that was held not to confer on a Scottish noble the right to a seat in the House of Lords. In 1712 legislation was passed to restore episcopalian modes of worship and to regulate lay patronage of episcopalian livings. In 1713 there was dissatisfaction about taxation and especially the malt tax. The first Jacobite rebellion of 1715 led to restrictive legislation, much of which was intended to ensure continuing allegiance to the Hanoverian line.

Central government was essentially in London, especially after the abolition of the Scottish Privy Council in 1708. Responsibility rested with the northern Secretary of State until 1782, when the matter passed to the Home Secretary assisted by the Lord Advocate. In practice the latter had great control, most notably Henry Dundas, later Viscount Melville from 1783 to 1806.

If much legal work was carried out in the Court of Session it did not prove to be the court of final determination. Just as major political decisions were passed to London, so legal appeals could competently go south to the House of Lords: *Greenshields v Magistrates of Edinburgh* (1710–1711).

The chief constitutional change, however, was the abolition, in breach of the Treaty of Union, of heritable jurisdictions in 1748 with substantial sums being paid to noblemen by way of compensation for their rights of justiciary. The power and prestige of the sheriff courts advanced steadily, and in 1747 the qualified sheriff depute replaced the hereditary officer and became the sheriff of the county. In 1828 the title depute was dropped and in 1971 the sheriff became the sheriff principal. In 1787 the office of sheriff substitute was recognised and made a salaried office. From 1825 the sheriff substitute was required to be a trained lawyer and in 1877 the office became a distinct Crown appointment.

The latter part of the eighteenth century is noted for the brilliant intellectual developments constituting the Scottish Enlightenment, a period of outstanding thinking and innovative writing in several disciplines. Further, institutional work came from John Erskine of Carnock (1695–1768). His *Principles of the Law of Scotland* (1754) and *Institute of the Law of Scotland* (published posthumously in 1773) displayed the classical Scots law, essentially deduced from principle, and resting on Roman law and feudal custom. Mention must also be made of Lord Kaimes (1696–1792), whose output was enormous and included *Principles of Equity* (1760), which proceeded with comparative references from English law.

THE NINETEENTH CENTURY

The transformation of Britain during this century was immense with enormous economic and social developments, and yet the central government was slow to alter. The Home Secretary was nominally the Minister responsible for Scotland, although the Lord Advocate of the day exercised great influence and patronage. The creation of the post of Secretary for Scotland (later the Secretary of State for Scotland) in 1885 brought about a new era, especially with the broadening of the franchise by the Reform Act of the same year.

The House of Lords heard many Scots appeals over the century, even though there was a lack of knowledge and experience of Scots law and a marked indifference on the part of the law lords. The most notable example was the imposition in Scots law of the doctrine of common employment, in the course of which Lord Cranworth said that "if such be the law of England, on what ground can it be argued not to be the law of Scotland?": *Bartonhill Coal Co v Reid* (1858) at 285.

Such a crass approach could not continue and in order to have a Scots lawyer in the House of Lords in 1866 Lord President McNeill was appointed as Lord Colonsay. He died in 1874. The Appellate Jurisdiction Act 1876 provided for salaried Lords of Appeal in Ordinary with life peerages. Since then there has always been at least one Scots lawyer, and usually two, in the Upper Chamber.

The Court of Session was also in need of reform as it had remained unchanged from its foundation to 1800. The reforms of 1808 divided the Inner House into the First and Second Divisions with lords ordinary in the Outer House preparing cases for hearings in the Inner House. Procedural changes diminished the role of written pleadings: Court of Session Act 1850. The use of shorthand notes improved and expedited business: Court of Session Act 1868.

The consolidation of the legal system in the nineteenth century extended to the legal profession. The introduction of the rank and dignity of Queen's Counsel in 1892 reflected the hierarchical view of society then and divided the Bar into senior and junior counsel. The Law Agents Act 1873 introduced examinations as a prerequisite for qualification as solicitor and the growth in graduates entering the profession was also unstable.

The institutional texts appearing in this period were principally David Hume's *Commentaries on the Law of Scotland respecting Crimes* (1756–1838) and George Joseph Bell's *Commentaries on the Law of Scotland and on the Principles of Mercantile Jurisprudence* (1770–1843). It is also a matter of comment that several judges wrote important textbooks. Lord McLaren wrote the standard book on *Wills and Succession* and Lord Fraser produced *Husband and Wife, Parent and Child* and also *Master and Servant.*

THE MODERN PERIOD

The huge growth in the volume and importance of public law matters such as public health, housing, town and country planning, social security, taxation and commerce resulted in new legislation unrelated to the older principles of Scots law. Moreover, the development of private law has also led to a statutory modification of common law doctrines. English influence has increased often in an insidious manner where legislation is carried out in great bulk. Changed conditions such as major wars and then peace have accentuated the need for change and the consequent development. The overall tendency has been to regulate society and individuals to a greater extent than previously.

The courts too have been increasingly reformed: in criminal law modern conditions rendered solemn procedure (with trial by jury) unsuitable for many of the offences created by Parliament. Procedure was rationalised by the Criminal Procedure Act 1887 which greatly simplified indictments, an approach extended to the summary criminal courts by the Summary Jurisdiction Act 1907, both of which are now consolidated in the Criminal Procedure (Scotland) Act 1995. In the civil courts procedure was simplified by the consolidating Act of Sederunt of 1913, itself superseded by the Rules of Court of 1936 (now 1994). The position and constitution of the Supreme Court was consolidated in the Court of Session Act 1988. Simplified procedure was introduced by the Sheriff Courts Act 1907 and 1971 for the sheriff court.

The continuing membership by the United Kingdom of the European Union maintains an additional and higher level of legal regulation. The political and legal balance within the United Kingdom in regard to the home jurisdictions of England and Wales, Northern Ireland and Scotland has emerged over the centuries. That legal balance has been tested with the development of rights and duties in regard to the European Union.

Moreover, with Royal Assent being given on November 19, 1998 to the Scotland Act 1998 a new factor is introduced into the legal equation. While law in the broad sense is adjusted for the United Kingdom in regard to the European Union, law within the jurisdictions of the United Kingdom will change following the establishment of a Scottish Parliament and a Welsh Assembly.

The establishment of the Scottish Parliament on July 1, 1999 marked a clear and decisive moment in the development of the Scottish legal system. The close physical proximity of a legislative body made a practical difference. The manner in which Members of the Scottish Parliament are elected, the extent to which it can control its own proceedings and the freedom to legislate on important subjects all mark out the Scottish Parliament from that of the United Kingdom.

---

2. THE SOURCES OF SCOTS LAW

The phrase "sources of law", as it is variously applied, indicates the various origins of the body of rules that is known as law. It is intended here to identify the principal sources and outline how it is that they give rise to law. First, there are historical sources of law. These derive from events or incidents in legal history which have given rise to the principle or rule in question. These can be ancient customs, Roman law, the Bible, canon law, feudal society or constitutional events. These historical sources of law explain the origins of a law but that law need not necessarily draw any validity or binding force from the individual source.

Secondly, legal rules and principles do not merely appear fully formed. They may be said to have social, political or economic sources or to be influenced strongly by religious or moral considerations. Most principles or rules of law have some such origin but with the passage of time and the varying importance of them the actual origins are often forgotten. The fact that a justification has been forgotten does not mean that the validity of that rule loses full force.

Thirdly, the commonest use of the phrase "source of law" is that which refers to the materials used to formulate a decision. The formal sources vary with the individual legal system and, consequently, Scots lawyers may view their sources as being different from other lawyers elsewhere. The relevant materials, discussed later, include legislation and precedent.

Fourthly, there is a group of rules which, although not actually law, are very similar to law and these may be said to be informal sources or quasi-sources.

FORMAL SOURCES

The formal sources of Scots law may be divided conveniently into major and minor sources, with informal sources being considered separately.

Major formal sources can be said to be legislation (such as European Union legislation, Acts of the United Kingdom Parliament and delegated legislation) and precedent (being the rules produced from practice in the courts).

Minor formal sources can be said to be prerogative legislation (legislation produced by the Crown but which has not gone through Parliament), institutional works (the writing, usually textbooks, of individuals) and, perhaps, custom (practices of people).

Major formal sources

A central question: where do I find the law which the courts will apply to determine the rights and duties of citizens or to clarify their remedies and liabilities? A simple answer might be that the only proper sources of legal principles and rules are the legal sources which are formal, because they give force to statements of law.

A legal source is one recognised by the legal system itself as a reservoir of valid authoritative and binding principles and rules of law. A legal source is one to which there may be resort to find the principle or rule of law to resolve a legal problem.

In the Scottish legal system the major formal sources are legislation and precedent. The emphasis to be put on each or either of these varies with the problem for which one seeks a solution. Legislation must, of course, be followed, as must precedent, but the role of judges in interpreting these sources allows for a degree of flexibility. In other legal systems approaches vary between civil law systems and common law systems.

Civil law systems were profoundly influenced in their development by Roman law and, in general, are codified in the sense that much of the law is set out in logical, reasoned and encyclopaedic form. The legal rules in civilian systems derive from codes, and the underlying principles of the system are also to be found in the codes. The central place of the codes results in the absence of the rule of precedent.

Common law systems are greatly influenced by English law, which was little affected by Roman law. The development of common law was due mainly but not exclusively to precedent, reflecting the decisions of courts. Common law systems tend not to have pivotal documents such as codes, and rules or principles are to be found in the decisions of the courts.

A third group of systems, a very small group, is that of mixed or hybrid systems and Scots law is a member of that group. There is an early and important influence of Roman law in Scots law and a later and no less important reliance on precedent as a source of law. The result is that there are discernible elements of the civil law and the common law approach in Scots law.

The legislation that constitutes part of the major formal source of Scots law is that part of the law that is deliberately and officially created, officially in the sense that it has passed through a legislature. Legislation thus varies over time and can be passed on an ad hoc basis. Each part of the legislation deals with an element of a particular subject matter and there is no encyclopaedic code.

The precedent that reflects common law influences arises from court cases where specific, and frequently unique, facts give rise to disputes or doubts as to what the law is. A precedent can change the law or the course of the development of the law. Underlying principles are to be found in precedent at common law rather than in legislation. Legislation can overrule, modify or complement common law precedent.

Minor formal sources

The first such source for consideration is that of prerogative legislation. While the great bulk of legislation requires to pass through Parliament by one of the various procedures, there is a limited residual power lying with the Crown to legislate without immediate reference to power. It must be said for the avoidance of doubt that the Crown in this context refers to the Government and not to the sovereign personally.

There is no general right on the part of the Crown to legislate: *Grieve v Edinburgh and District Water Trustees* (1918). The right to legislate arises in regard to specific topics. A recent example is the authority given by s.1 of the United Nations Act 1946 to enact such provisions as appear necessary or expedient for the apprehension, trial and punishment of persons offending against the Charter of the United Nations. This led to the High Court of Justiciary (Proceedings in the Netherlands) Order 1998, which facilitated the conducting of criminal proceedings under Scots law in the Netherlands. This Order, an Order in Council, was made by the sovereign on the advice of the Privy Council. Prerogative legislation may have different names and styles, for example Letters Patent, Royal Instructions, Proclamations and Royal Warrant. The extent to which the sovereign and the Privy Council are involved probably varies with each Order in Council as the Government instigates the procedure.

The second minor formal source is the body of literary work known as books of authority or the institutional writers. The diverse and anachronistic sources of law in the seventeenth century encouraged a more systematic treatment of the law and that was as true for Scotland as it was for other parts of Europe. Indeed, a general model which proved to be highly influential was the *corpus juris civilis*, by which late Roman law was codified in the sixth century. Two parts of the codification were the *Digest* (or the *Pandect*) and the *Institutiones*. In the former a reconciliation was attempted of the commentaries on the major Roman legal matters of previous centuries. In the latter there was a general introduction to Roman law.

The systematic treatment of Scots law beginning in the mid-seventeenth century produced several major works which adopted the title institutes or institutions following the approach of Roman law. The importance of these works of Scots law in the past lay in the principle that a statement of the law in them, in default of higher authority, was almost certainly taken as settling the law: see, *e.g. Drew v Drew* (1870) at 167, where Lord Benholme says: "[w]hen on any point of law I find Stair's opinion uncontradicted I look upon that opinion as ascertaining the Law of Scotland". Under modern conditions the statements of the institutional writers are likely to remain influential but, perhaps, not quite so authoritative; see *Shillingday v Smith* (1998) for an example of Stair's *Institutions* being cited recently.

The authority of statements in institutional writings depends on recognition by the courts and probably equates with a decision of either Division of the Inner House: see D.M. Walker, *The Scottish Legal System* (8th ed.), p.457. Institutional writings may also be referred to as authority reinforcing older judicial decisions: *Morgan Guaranty Trust Co v Lothian R.C.* (1995). Courts have approved and disapproved of statements on the same particular points in different institutional writings in the same case, *e.g. Burns v H.M. Advocate* (1995).

Not every book by an institutional writer is accorded institutional status. Each institutional writer, however, is recognised for at least one principal work: the best known on civil matters is Lord Stair's *The Institutions of the Law of Scotland* (1681), and on criminal matters is Baron Hume's *Commentaries on the Law of Scotland Respecting Crimes* (1797).

The third minor formal source is custom. This was historically a very important source of law but it now plays a much smaller part. There may be at least three reasons for the reduced importance of custom as such a source. First, many older customs became embodied in the writings of the institutional writers. Secondly, there has been an increasing amount of parliamentary activity resulting in custom being overshadowed greatly by formal legislation. Thirdly, modern conditions militate against the type of habit that developed into custom.

Custom, however, may still be assessed and, if proved, may be a valid source of a new rule of law. Four conditions, at least, require to be met for a custom to be accepted as a source of law. First, a custom must be an exception to, yet still consistent with, the existing general body of law: *McCann v Anderson* (1981). Secondly, the custom must be definite and certain. Thirdly, the custom must be fair and reasonable: *Bruce v Smith* (1890). Finally, the custom must have been generally accepted for long enough to justify the inference that it has long been accepted as law. No particular period of time must be proved: Erskine, *An Institute of the Law of Scotland* (1773), Vol.1, p.44. Customs may fall into desuetude, that is lose authority by contrary usage: *Royal Four Towns Fishing Association v Dumfriesshire Assessor* (1956).

INFORMAL OR QUASI-SOURCES

The major and minor formal sources of law discussed earlier may be contrasted with informal or quasi-sources. The latter group may be said to be a substantial and rather imprecise collection of rules and principles which are associated with law or abided by as if law although they do not fit into the categories of the formal sources. The first element of the informal sources is constitutional conventions. Constitutional law can be divided into two main groups: rules of law derived from statute, decided cases and custom; and a body of rules, understandings, habits or practices which are not in strictness rules of law, in the sense that they will not be enforced by the courts, commonly termed conventions of the constitution.

These conventional rules and practices are of intense interest to political historians and political scientists and also to lawyers because they affect the rules for the operation of government usually at the highest level. Constitutional conventions are all the more important given the absence of a written constitution in the United Kingdom.

Constitutional conventions are not enforceable by the courts, but this does not undermine their importance because without such conventions the constitutional machinery would probably be unworkable.

The second element of the informal sources will, paradoxically, cease in time to be such. The Convention for the Protection of Human Rights and Fundamental Freedoms (the European Convention on Human Rights) was drafted by Member States of the Council of Europe and has been ratified by the United Kingdom. It requires its signatories to secure certain specified human rights such as a right to life, a right to liberty and freedom from torture or inhuman or degrading treatment. For many years these rights were not strictly part of the law in the United Kingdom although the signatories were obliged to ensure that their legislation was compatible with the Convention. One might more properly say that the substantive rights guaranteed by the Convention could not be enforced in the national courts: those said to have been breached required to be enforced indirectly. One such way was by application, where the remedies in the ordinary courts had been exhausted, to the European Commission on Human Rights. In the absence of a friendly statement, the Commission had the power to refer the case to the European Court of Human Rights: see, *e.g. Campbell and Cosans v. UK* (1982).

The rights and freedoms envisaged or promoted by the European Convention were not for many years interpreted into the law in the United Kingdom. The result was that the rights and freedoms might only be enforced in the courts, in Scotland at least, in so far as they were embodied in existing rights: see generally *Kaur v Lord Advocate* (1981) and *Moore v Secretary of State* (1985). In recent years, however, a different approach developed. In *Anderson v H.M. Advocate* (1996) it was observed, *per* Lord Justice-General Hope (at 131–132) that provisions such as these might not be part of domestic law but the principles involved had for long been such.

In relevant domains, the European Convention on Human Rights could be enforced through the law of the European Union. The European Court of Justice held that the fundamental freedoms of human rights were an integral part of the general law of what is now the European Union: *Internationale Handelgesellschaft* (1970). Moreover, the treaties on human rights supplied guidelines to be followed within the law of the European Union: *Nold v E.G. Commission* (1974).

The implementation of the European Convention on Human Rights as part of the law of the United Kingdom by the Human Rights Act 1998 ends human rights treaties or conventions as a quasi-source of rules or principles which are not unequivocally law.

The third element of informal sources of rules and principles is administrative guidance. This is frequently but not invariably from government departments. The guidance is expected, at most, or intended, at least, to be acted upon and to that extent regulates the activities of citizens or civil servants as law might do.

One of the clearest examples of administrative guidance is that of the Highway Code. The normative aspect of the Code is evident through the guidance and illustrations. The enforceability of the Code is emphasised by s.38 of the Road Traffic Act 1988, which provides that a breach of the Code does not amount to an offence but may be relied on in civil or criminal proceedings to establish liability.

Other examples of informal sources include professional codes of conduct and Government circulars, *e.g.* from Crown Office circulars issued to procurators fiscal carrying instructions on a given point from the Lord Advocate. These may find their authority in statutory provisions but that is not always so. Enforcement of these documents can often be indirect so that to ignore the administrative guidance is to run the risk, for example, of having a decision set aside after judicial review.

---

3. COURTS AND TRIBUNALS

The adjudication of disputes or the resolving of conflicts and claims generally takes place in courts or tribunals sitting to deal with civil, administrative or criminal business. The civil and criminal courts are of great antiquity, although governed by modern legislation. The special courts and statutory tribunals are much more modern.

Courts are divided into superior and inferior categories: the former courts have jurisdiction over the whole country, the latter over only a particular district. Courts and tribunals are divided into those having original jurisdiction, dealing with disputes for the first time, or appellate jurisdiction, dealing with disputes appealed from some other forum. There are some courts that have both original and appellate jurisdiction. The various courts are considered in descending order of authority.

CIVIL COURTS: GENERAL JURISDICTION

House of Lords

The House of Lords has original jurisdiction only in cases of impeachment, breach of privileges and, acting on the recommendation of its Committee of Privileges, in relation to disputed claims to a peerage: see, *e.g. Earldom of Annandale and Hartfell* (1986). The House of Lords has appellate jurisdiction to deal with appeals to the Queen in Parliament. The modern practice is for appeals to be heard only by the legally qualified members of the House, namely, the Lord Chancellor, the Lords of Appeal in Ordinary, and peers who hold or have held high judicial office, sitting as an Appellate Committee of the House. The number of Lords of Appeal has increased from two in 1876 to 12 in recent years: Appellate Jurisdiction Act 1995. The quorum is three but appeals are frequently heard by five and sometimes, in the more serious cases, by seven Law Lords. The decision is by a majority. In consequence of this the unanimous decisions of judges in the Court of Session may be reversed by a majority of one in the House of Lords. There have been cases in the past where the House of Lords, sitting with an even number of Law Lords, has been divided equally, in which instance the appeal failed: *Commercial Union Assurance v Waddell* (1919); *Kennedy v Spratt* (1972).

In recent years it has been the custom to have at any time two Law Lords of Scottish origin, in the sense that they obtained a legal qualification and practised predominantly in Scotland. Other judges in Scotland who are peers have occasionally assisted in the hearing of appeals.

It is competent for Law Lords who have had no training in or experience of other jurisdictions in the United Kingdom to deal with appeals from those other jurisdictions. Thus, a majority of English Law Lords heard the Scottish appeal of *Grant v Sun Shipping Co Ltd* (1948). In *Arenson v Casson Beckman Rutley & Co* (1975) a majority of Scottish Law Lords heard an English appeal.

By legal fiction the House of Lords, as the final Court of Appeal for England, Northern Ireland and Scotland, has judicial knowledge of all the legal systems involved so that it can take cognisance of points of law of each of these systems, even though these points have not been argued or established by the evidence before it: *Cooper v Cooper* (1888); *Elliott v Joicey* (1935).

The actual hearing of the appeals is within a committee room of the House and not the actual chamber. The Lords do not wear judicial robes but members of the Bar are robed. The Lords, however, do sit in the chamber when they vote on the motion put by the Lord Chancellor or senior Law Lord that the appeal be allowed or dismissed. The actual judgments are speeches in support of or against the motion and were delivered orally in the past. Now the judgments are issued in typescript and the Lords merely announce that the appeal will be allowed or dismissed for reasons stated separately. Decisions need not be unanimous but if the Law Lords are divided equally the appeal fails. Split decisions or other problems may result in the House ordering a case to be re-argued: see, *e.g. Bannatyne v Lord Overtoun* (1904), although these results are rare now.

Appeals to the House of Lords are competent both on fact and law, though appeals on fact are not regarded favourably and great weight is attached by the House to the views on the evidence of the trial judge who saw and heard the witnesses: *Thomas v Thomas* (1947). If the case originated in the sheriff court the right of appeal is limited to questions of law: Court of Session Act 1988 ("1988 Act"), s.32(5), but see *Martinez v Grampian Health Board* (1996).

Appeal may be taken without leave of the Inner House against final judgments of the Inner House which dispose of the action, including judgments in Exchequer cases, or against interlocutory judgments which dispose of some part or stage of the action, if the judges were not unanimous. Appeal is competent where the interlocutory judgment sustained a dilatory defence and dismissed the action, or with leave of the Inner House against any other interlocutory judgment: *McIntosh v British Railways Board* (1990); *Ferguson v Maclennan Salmon Co* (1990). An interlocutor granting or refusing a new jury trial is appealable without leave.

It is incompetent to appeal against an interlocutor of a Lord Ordinary unless it has been reviewed in the Inner House: 1988 Act, s.40. No appeal is allowed to the House of Lords against a decision of the Court of Session on an appeal relating to estate duty except with the leave of the court: 1988 Act, s.52(3).

The decision of the House of Lords is not an operative judgment because the matter is returned to the Court of Session with the decision of the House of Lords. The successful party must then petition the Court of Session for a decree which applies that judgment.

Judicial Committee of the Privy Council

The Judicial Committee of the Privy Council (with offices at No. 1 Downing Street, Westminster) was historically the supreme court of appeal for British colonies, dependencies and other overseas terrirories, and more recently for commonwealth countries. The final right of appeal to the Judicial Committee has been abolished by most countries leaving a restricted jurisdiction. The United Kingdom Government, however, decided at the time of devolution that the Judicial Committee was to be the court of last resort for determining devolution issues of two types.

First, the Scotland Act 1998 provided by s.33 that the Advocate General, the Lord Advocate or the Attorney General may refer the question of whether a Bill or any provision in a Bill would be within the legislative competence of the Scottish Parliament to the Judicial Committee for a decision. Where the Judicial Committee determines that a particular provision or a whole Bill is not within the legislative competence of the Scottish Parliament than amendment is necessary before the matter may be submitted for Royal Assent.

Secondly, the Judicial Committee may be required to determine "devolution issues": these are issues, for example, of whether the purported or proposed exercise of a function by a member of the Scottish Executive is, or would be, incompatible with any of the Convention rights or with Community law: see Scotland Act 1998, s.98 and Sch.6 for full definitions. If a devolution issue arises in a court of first instance, it may be referred to the Inner House of the Court of Session or the High Court of Justiciary as appropriate for determination. Appeals against such decisions will lie to the Judicial Committee.

To ensure the effectiveness of the Judicial Committee in this aspect of the law, the decisions of the Judicial Committee are binding on the Scottish courts: Scotland Act 1998, s.103(1)

Court of Session

The Court of Session is a superior court having jurisdiction over the whole of Scotland and it has both original and appellate jurisdiction.

Judges are designated Senators of the College of Justice or Lords of Council and Session. In court they wear dark blue robes with maroon facings and scarlet crosses on those facings. The judges sit in Parliament House in Edinburgh to hear civil business there.

The judges of the Court of Session sat together in the Inner House as a collegiate court from 1521 to 1808. During that long period one or two judges heard the preliminary stages of cases and did so for a week at a time in the Outer House.

In the reforms of 1808 the court was divided into two divisions chaired by the Lord President and the Lord Justice-Clerk respectively. In the reforms of 1825 the Divisions were reduced to four judges each (including those in the chair) and the remaining seven judges became Lords Ordinary sitting only in the Outer House.

The judges of the old court, before 1808, were known as the "haill fifteen" but the maximum number of judges is now 26. The Lord President with the consent of the Secretary of State may appoint a retired Court of Session judge or Lord of Appeal who is not yet 75 years old to be a temporary judge. Any person eligible for appointment as a judge of the Court of Session may be appointed a temporary judge for as long as the Secretary of State may determine but not beyond his or her 75th birthday.

The court has extensive powers by Act of Sederunt to regulate its own procedure and practice: 1988 Act, s.5. The court has exclusive jurisdiction in some matters such as actions of reduction but otherwise a pursuer is left to decide whether to bring an action in the Court of Session or the sheriff court.

The Inner House
Any party to a cause commenced in the Outer House may appeal or reclaim against the interlocutor of the Lord Ordinary to the Inner House: 1988 Act, s.28.

The Inner House now has two Divisions of equal authority and jurisdiction. The Lord President and three senior Lords of Session constitute the First Division. The Lord Justice-Clerk and three other Lords of Session sit in the Second Division. In ordinary practice only three of the four sit in court and that is a quorum. In extraordinary cases the four judges will sit.

In order to constitute a quorum either Division may call in a judge from the Outer House or from the other Division. A vacancy, such as through retirement, arising in either Division was filled formerly by the appointment of the senior Lord Ordinary, and now by a Lord Ordinary appointed by the Lord President and the Lord Justice-Clerk with the consent of the Secretary of State and after such consultation as appears appropriate: Law Reform (Miscellaneous Provisions) (Scotland) Act 1990, Sch.4.

The Lord President may appoint any three judges to be an Extra Division to assist in dealing with Inner House business and a senior judge presides in that Extra Division. Moreover, in cases of real importance and difficulty the First and Second Divisions may sit together as a court of seven judges, or may summon additional judges to constitute a larger court: 1988 Act, s.36.

The Inner House is a court of first instance in special cases (where the facts are admitted and a judicial opinion is sought) and revenue stated cases. It is generally, however, a court of appeal for matters from the sheriff court and the Outer House and other tribunals. An appeal is competent to the Inner House after trial by civil jury: 1988 Act, s.29.

It is very unusual for evidence to be heard in the Inner House but if that is done then only one judge hears it and then reports to the remaining judges of the Division: 1988 Act, s.37. The greater part of Inner House business is disposed of on hearing argument on the law applicable to proved, admitted or undisputed facts.

The two Divisions of the Inner House rank equally and there is no formal distinction between them. Whatever the position in the past, prospective litigants cannot choose a Division to hear an appeal. Exchequer causes at all times take precedence over all other causes in the court. In these types of case the Lord Advocate, on behalf of the Crown, has the privilege of being heard last: 1988 Act, ss.21 to 24.

The Outer House

The judges, the Lords of Session, now sit to hear cases at first instance. A jury of 12 is competent and used increasingly. Prospective litigants cannot now choose a judge to hear a case. The jurisdiction of the Outer House extends to all kinds of civil claims unless jurisdiction is expressly excluded by statute. One judge is now seconded to act as chairman of the Scottish Law Commission and does not sit judicially full-time. One of the judges who does sit judicially full-time is appointed to act as Lord Ordinary in Exchequer causes: 1988 Act, s.3. One judge is appointed full-time as commercial judge while others are appointed part-time to deal with commercial cases. The remaining judges deal with a large volume of business, of a legal and administrative nature, that does not proceed on appeal to the Inner House. In certain cases actions commenced in the sheriff court may be remitted to the Court of Session.

Sheriff court

Scotland is divided into six sheriffdoms based on the groupings of local government areas. The present sheriffdoms are: Lothian and Borders; South Strathclyde, Dumfries and Galloway; Glasgow and Strathkelvin; North Strathclyde; Tayside, Central and Fife; and Grampian, Highlands and Islands.

Each sheriffdom has a sheriff principal who has the general duty of securing the speedy and efficient disposal of business in the courts of the sheriffdom. Each sheriffdom is divided into several sheriff court districts centred on a town where there is a sheriff court.

Each sheriffdom also has several sheriffs who are qualified lawyers in Scotland. The number of sheriffs varies greatly, depending on the place and the extent of legal business: thus, in Glasgow there are in excess of 20 sheriffs whereas Orkney and Shetland have one sheriff between them.

The organisation and administration of the courts is the function of the Scottish Courts Administration and the Scottish Court Service. These bodies can also provide sheriffs principal with full-time "floating" sheriffs or temporary sheriffs where such immediate assistance is necessary. Sheriffs principal may appoint legally qualified honorary sheriffs to assist occasionally.

Unlike the criminal jurisdiction, in civil business the sheriff court is both a court of first instance and a court of appeal. Certain appeals such as those involving licensing and firearms and from decisions of children's hearings are taken to the sheriff. Some cases heard by a sheriff may competently be appealed to the sheriff principal.

The civil jurisdiction of the sheriff court is wide and encompasses actions of debt or damages without any pecuniary limit. There may from time to time be actions involving substantial sums of money. There may also be actions based on contract, delict and a wide variety of family matters.

Certain matters may be initiated in the sheriff court but for reasons of complexity or general public concern they may be remitted to the Court of Session. Actions of divorce or for settling the custody or adoption of children may be remitted to the Court of Session by the sheriff alone: Sheriff Courts (Scotland) Act 1971, s.37(2A).

In contrast, jurisdiction in the sheriff court is exclusive and final in cases where the value of the action does not exceed £1,500. Special procedure applies to claims not exceeding £1,500 brought under the summary cause rules or the small claims rules.

The Court of Session originally had exclusive jurisdiction over all actions involving status but divorce is now a competent action in the sheriff court: Divorce Jurisdiction Court Fees and Legal Aid (Scotland) Act 1983, s.1. The Court of Session alone deals with actions of inhibitions, adjudication and reduction, and proving the tenor of lost documents.

Appeal lies in civil matters by note of appeal without leave (*i.e.* without first obtaining the permission of the court) against final judgments and with leave against interlocutory (*i.e.* interim) judgments from the sheriff to the sheriff principal, or to the Inner House of the Court of Session, or to the sheriff principal and then from his decision to the Inner House of the Court of Session: Sheriff Courts (Scotland) Act 1907, ss.27 to 29. In summary cases it lies to the sheriff principal by stated case raising questions of law, and no other matters may be raised; see *Kostric v O'Hara* (1990). Thereafter, an appeal may go to the Court of Session on a point of law from the final judgment of the sheriff principal if he certifies it as suitable for such an appeal: 1971 Act, s.38. In small claims appeal cannot proceed beyond the sheriff principal: Law Reform (Miscellaneous Provisions) (Scotland) Act 1980, s.18.

CIVIL COURTS: SPECIAL JURISDICTION

Court of the Lord Lyon

This court illustrates clearly the jurisdiction of this category of courts to consider particular kinds of claims only. The Lord Lyon King of Arms exercises the whole Crown jurisdiction in armorial matters and similar subjects. He is controller of messengers-at-arms and head of the department of Scots law concerned with execution and diligence. The Court of the Lord Lyon exercises both a civil and criminal jurisdiction and in the latter he has a procurator fiscal who acts as public prosecutor: *MacDonald of Keppoch, Petr* (1989).

Court of Teinds

The Court of Teinds has its own procedure and a Teind Clerk. It consists of the eight Inner House judges along with the second junior Lord Ordinary. The quorum is five. Teinds were previously the tenth part of the output of the land and labour given for the maintenance of church and clergy. Now most of the business of the court proceeds without opposition.

Court of Exchequer

This court now deals mainly with appeals on law by way of stated case against the determination of the Special Commissioners of Income Tax in regard to liability for tax. Although long ago a separate court, it is now the Court of Session sitting as the Court of Exchequer in Scotland. A further appeal lies to the House of Lords.

Lands Valuation Appeal Court

This court consists of one judge or, where he directs or where the appeal is against a determination of the Lands Tribunal for Scotland in a valuation case, three judges of the Court of Session: Rating and Valuation (Amendment) (Scotland) Act 1984, s.13. The court disposes of appeals against the determination of the local Valuation Appeal Committee or the Lands Tribunal as to the value to be set on heritable property for the purpose of raising local rates.

Valuation Appeal Committees are required to state cases for appeals: *Lugano v Ayrshire Valuation Appeal Committee* (1972). The stated case sets out the facts held to be proved or admitted before the committee and the relevant questions of law. The issue in appeals tends to be more statutory interpretation than actual valuations. This appeal court is final and there is no appeal to the House of Lords.

Scottish Land Court

This court, as its name suggests, is concerned with agriculture. The four members of the court, other than the chairman, are necessarily experienced in agriculture. The chairman is a lawyer having the status and tenure of a judge of the Court of Session. The annual report of the court is laid before Parliament.

The jurisdiction of the court is entirely statutory: Small Landholders (Scotland) Act 1911; Agricultural Holdings (Scotland) Act 1949; Scottish Land Court Act 1993. An appeal from the Scottish Land Court lies with the Inner House of the Court of Session by stated case on a point of law: Crofters (Scotland) Act 1961, s.4.

Statutory tribunals

The Tribunals and Inquiries Act 1971 followed on an earlier Act which had given effect to some of the recommendations of the Franks Committee on Administrative Tribunals and Inquiries, Cmnd. 218 (1957). The Act provided that the chairman of certain tribunals specified in the Act had to be selected by the appropriate Minister from panels appointed by the Lord President and no person's membership of any of the tribunals listed in the Schedule to the Act might be ended without the approval of the Lord President.

Scheduled tribunals are required when requested to give reasons for their decisions, unless exempted from such requirement. National security may justify such reasons being withheld. The Act also enlarged the number of tribunals from which appeal lay on a point of law to the Court of Session.

The Council on Tribunals was established, again following a recommendation of the Franks Committee, and it consists of from 10 to

15 members appointed by the Lord Chancellor and the Lord Advocate, one of whom is chairman. It has a Scottish Committee of two or three members, together with three or four non-members appointed by the Lord Advocate. The Parliamentary Commissioner for Administration is ex officio a member of the Council and of its Scottish Committee. All members are part-time and they are not necessarily lawyers.

The Council keeps under consideration the constitution and working of the tribunals listed in the Schedule to the 1971 Act: see the 1971 Act, Sched. 1, Pts 1 and 2. Particular matters may be referred to the Council by the Lord Chancellor and the Lord Advocate to consider and report. The Council makes an annual report to the Lord Chancellor and the Lord Advocate.

Classifying the many statutory tribunals is very difficult because of the widely varying nature of their subjects and involvement. One attempt has been made to list the tribunals of substantial importance: D. M. Walker, *The Scottish Legal System* (8th ed., 2001), pp.301 *et seq.* The categories are the revenue group (Bookmakers' Levy, Commissioners of Income Tax, Value Added Tax Tribunal), the social security group (Independent Tribunal Service, War Pensions, Social Security Appeals Tribunals, Child Support Appeal Tribunal), the health group (Inefficient Practitioners, Complaints Tribunal, Misuse of Drugs Tribunal, Vaccine Damage Tribunal, Mental Welfare Commission, Mental Health Tribunal), the employment group (Industrial Tribunals (now Employment Tribunals), Employment Appeal Tribunal, Advisory, Conciliation and Arbitration Service, Central Arbitration Committee), and the land group (Agricultural Holdings, Crofters Commission, Forestry Commission, Lands Tribunal for Scotland, Rent Assessment Committee, Valuation, Building Control and Planning Control).

There is also the transport group (the Traffic Commissioner, Transport Tribunal, Civil Aviation), the commercial group (Banking Tribunal, Financial Services Tribunal, Building Societies Tribunal and the Insolvency Practitioners Tribunal), the intellectual property group (Patents, Industrial Design, Trade Marks, Plant Varieties and Copyright) and the deceptively named miscellaneous group (Children's Hearings, Immigration, Data Protection, Liquor Licensing, Licensing of Betting, Gaming and Lotteries, Consumer Credit Businesses and Schools).

Each of these committees or tribunals has a separate listing and has a different composition with varying powers and appeals. There are no settled rules as to right of appeal from their decisions although the sheriff is authorised by many statutes to order matters to be done or to hear appeals from these committees or tribunals. It is necessary, therefore, to consider the governing legislation for each appeal to discern what may competently be done.

This may amount to reaching a new decision or remitting the case back for reconsideration, *e.g. Botterills of Blantyre v Hamilton District Licensing Board* (1986). There may also be a further appeal to the Court of Session, either by way of appeal or by stated case on a point of law, *e.g. Kaye v Hunter* (1958). Where a right of appeal to the sheriff is given and the statute gives no indication about review of his or her decision then the presumption is that the sheriff's decision is final: *T v Secretary of State for Scotland* (1987). A sheriff has no right to exercise judicial review, unless jurisdiction is conferred specifically: *Brown v Hamilton D.C.* (1983).

Fatal Accident Inquiries

Procurators Fiscal, with a duty to report to the Lord Advocate, are required to investigate all sudden, suspicious and unexplained deaths that occur within the district for which that Procurator Fiscal is responsible. these investigations mostly conclude administratively, that is to say, privately and without the need for a public hearing. Public hearings are required in certain circumstances and these Fatal Accident Inquiries are civil hearings with the appropriate rules of evidence to be applied.

There are mandatory Fatal Accident Inquiries, generally speaking, where a person dies while in lawful custody and where a person is killed in the course of his or her employment. There are discretionary inquiries where it appears to the Lord Advocate to be expedient in the public interest that such a public hearing takes place. at the conclusion of such a Fatal Accident Inquiry the Sheriff (who sits without a jury) issues a written determination and that document must set out the facts proved and may set out recommendations: see *Dekker*, 2000 S.C.L.R. 1087 where it was held that Fatal Accident Inquiries are not the appropriate forum for determining matters of civil or criminal liability.

CRIMINAL COURTS

House of Lords

The House of Lords has no general jurisdiction to hear criminal appeals from Scotland. There is no appeal from the High Court of Justiciary to the House of Lords: *Macintosh v Lord Advocate* (1876), especially *per* Lord Cairns, L.C. at 36. Moreover, it has been asserted again recently that all interlocutors and sentences pronounced by the High Court of Justiciary are final and conclusive, and not subject to review by any court whatsoever: Criminal Procedure (Scotland) Act 1995, s.124(2).

The Courts-Martial (Appeals) Act 1968 provides that a Courts-Martial Appeal Court in Scotland shall consist of such Lords Commissioner of Justiciary as the Lord Justice-General may nominate, being uneven in number and not less than three. In practice, admittedly rare, the rule is for the High Court of Justiciary sitting in its appellate capacity to sit as the Court-Martial Appeal Court, *e.g. R v Hendry* (1955). It is from that court that appeal lies to the House of Lords by leave of the court or of the House of Lords, which shall be granted only if the Court-Martial Appeal Court certifies that a point of law of general public importance is involved and that it appears to that court or the House of Lords that the point ought to be considered by the House of Lords: 1968 Act, s.39.

Judicial Committee of the Privy Council

A description of the duties of the Judicial Committee of the Privy Council under the civil courts applies to criminal courts also: the latter have produced many notable cases in recent years, *e.g. Brown v Stott*, 2001 S.L.T. 59.

High Court of Justiciary

This court was established in 1672 and it is now presided over by the Lord Justice-General. Down to 1836 various Scottish noblemen held the office of Lord Justice-General but since that year the office has been taken along with that of Lord President of the Court of Session.

The Lord Justice-Clerk was originally the clerk of the criminal court. The Lord Justice-Clerk became the normal president as the 1672 Act provided that he should preside when the Lord Justice-General did not sit, which was usually the case until the latter office ceased to be honorary.

In 1887 the court was established as consisting of the Lord Justice-General, the Lord Justice-Clerk, and the Lords of Session as Lords Commissioners of Justiciary. Temporary judges of the Court of Session are also temporary Lords Commissioners of Justiciary: Law Reform (Miscellaneous Provisions) (Scotland) Act 1990, Sch.4, para.8.

The High Court of Justiciary has jurisdiction over Scotland and in respect of all crimes, unless the jurisdiction of the court is excluded expressly or by implication by statute. The High Court of Justiciary also has jurisdiction outside Scotland in relation to acts or omissions outside the United Kingdom by any British citizen or British subject which would constitute the crime of murder or culpable homicide: Criminal Procedure (Scotland) Act 1995, s.11(2) (the "1995 Act").

The High Court of Justiciary is both a court at first instance and a court of appeal and has certain other legal duties. Accordingly, a detailed consideration might reasonably be dealt with under four separate headings.

1. High Court of Justiciary in its appellate capacity: solemn procedure

As a consequence of the Criminal Appeal (Scotland) Act 1926, which resulted in *Slater v H.M. Advocate* (1928), the jurisdiction of the High Court was extended to allow appeals against conviction and/or sentence after trial by jury before either a judge or a sheriff. Before this change no such appeal was competent. The appellate capacity gives rise to the court being described colloquially as "the Appeal Court" or "the Court of Criminal Appeal".

For appeals against sentence the court consists of three or more judges and the determination of any question is according to the majority of members of the court sitting, including the presiding judge, and each judge so sitting is entitled to pronounce a separate opinion: 1995 Act, s.103(2). A lesser quorum of two judges is competent to hear appeals against various sentences: 1995 Act, s.102(3).

Appeals are brought by written note of appeal stating all the grounds of appeal against conviction or against sentence or against both: 1995 Act, s.110(1). By appeal a person may also bring under review any alleged miscarriage of justice: 1995 Act, s.106(3). The court has very extensive powers to dispose of an appeal either in regard to conviction or sentence: 1995 Act, s.118(1) and (3). These powers include granting authority for a new prosecution: 1995 Act, s.118(1)(c).

The Lord Advocate has a right of appeal against a disposal. Such an appeal may be on a point of law or, alternatively, "where it appears to the Lord Advocate that the disposal was unduly lenient": 1995 Act, s.108(2)(a) and (b). There is also a power to allow the Lord Advocate to appeal against a decision not to impose an automatic sentence in certain cases: 1995 Act, s.108A.

It is not competent to appeal to the High Court of Justiciary by bill of suspension against any conviction, sentence, judgment or order made in any proceedings on an indictment in the sheriff court: 1995 Act, s.130. Appeal by bill of advocation remains competent. The prosecutor's right of appeal by means of a bill of advocation extends to the review of a decision of any court of solemn jurisdiction: 1995 Act, s.131(1).

2. High Court of Justiciary in its appellate capacity: summary procedure

Appeals from courts of summary criminal jurisdiction comprise appeals from the sheriff court or the district court. For appeals against conviction, the appellate court consists of three or more judges and the determination of any question is according to the majority of members of the court sitting, including the presiding judge, and each judge so sitting shall be entitled to pronounce a separate opinion: 1995 Act, s.173(1). A lesser quorum of two judges is competent to hear appeals against various sentences: 1995 Act, s.173(2).

Appeals may relate to conviction and/or sentence: 1995 Act, s.175. By appeal a person may also bring under review any alleged miscarriage of justice: 1995 Act, s.175(5). The mode of appeal in a summary matter is generally by stated case for which application must be made timeously: 1995 Act, s.176(1). A stated case shall be, as nearly as may be, in the form prescribed by Act of Adjournal: 1995 Act, s.178(2) and the Act of Adjournal (Criminal Procedure Rules) 1996, r. 19.2(2) and Form 19.2–B.

The court has extensive powers to dispose of an appeal either with regard to conviction or sentence: 1995 Act, s.183(1). These powers must include the authorising of new prosecutions: 1995 Act, s.185.

The prosecutor in summary proceedings may appeal to the High Court of Justiciary against a sentence passed on conviction: 1995 Act, s.175(4). However, a conviction or sentence may also be set aside with the prosecutor's consent or application: 1995 Act, s.188.

A party to a summary prosecution may in certain circumstances appeal to the High Court of Justiciary by bill of suspension against conviction or, as the case may be, by bill of advocation against an acquittal on the ground of an alleged miscarriage of justice: 1995 Act, s.191(1).

3. References to the court

The High Court of Justiciary sitting in its appellate capacity may be required to consider several types of reference: first where a person tried on indictment is acquitted or convicted of a charge, the Lord Advocate may refer a point of law which has risen in relation to the judge's charges to the jury in the High Court of Justiciary for their opinion on the law: 1995 Act, s.123(1).

Secondly, the Secretary of State on the consideration of any conviction of a person or the sentence passed on a person who has been convicted, may, if he thinks fit, at any time, and whether or not an appeal against such conviction or sentence has previously been heard and determined by the High Court of Justiciary, refer the whole case to the High Court of Justiciary and the case shall be heard and determined, subject to any directions the High Court of Justiciary may make, as if it were an appeal: 1995 Act, s.124(3).

An appeal against conviction and/or sentence under solemn or summary procedure is competent in the High Court of Justiciary sitting in its appellate capacity. In practice this means that appeals from the whole of Scotland are heard in Edinburgh.

4. High Court of Justiciary as trial court

The High Court of Justiciary sits as a court of first instance in Edinburgh to hear trials and it goes out on circuit as required. Scotland is divided into four circuits: Home, West, North and South. While some towns have regular sittings, the circuits are not restricted to these towns. A sitting may be held in any town which is convenient, given the circumstances of a particular crime.

Whatever the technical nature of the High Court of Justiciary sitting in Glasgow, in practice the court is there permanently with most judges taking turns to try cases there. However, the Lord Justice-General does not go on circuit and the Lord Justice-Clerk only goes out exceptionally.

In modern times only one judge sits at a trial but in cases of difficulty or importance two or more, usually three, may sit, if not for the whole trial then at least to hear debate on a point of difficulty: *e.g. Copeland v H.M. Advocate* (1987).

The procedure is always solemn: any crime or offence which is triable on indictment may be tried by the High Court of Justiciary sitting at any place in Scotland: 1995 Act, s.3(2).

Sheriff court

The sheriff court is the court of universal jurisdiction where it is competent to proceed both under solemn procedure and, separately, under summary procedure.

Trials under solemn procedure in the sheriff court proceed before a sheriff sitting with a jury. It is for the Crown alone to decide on that procedure, rather than summary procedure, and there is no right for an accused to elect trial by jury. The sheriff is entitled, on the conviction on indictment of an accused, to pass a sentence of imprisonment for a term of up to three years: 1995 Act, s.3(3). However, if a sheriff holds that any competent sentence which he or she can impose is inadequate so that the question of sentence is appropriate for the High Court of Justiciary, the accused may be remitted to appear in the higher court for sentence: 1995 Act, s.195(2). Generally, trials under solemn procedure in the High Court of Justiciary and the sheriff court follow identical rules: see the 1995 Act, ss.64 to 102.

Trials under summary procedure in the sheriff court proceed before a sheriff sitting alone. The sheriff has a power to imprison for a period not exceeding three months: 1995 Act, s.5(2)(d). That period is extended to one not exceeding six months where a person is convicted of a second or subsequent offence inferring dishonest appropriation of property or attempted dishonest appropriation of property, or a second or subsequent offence inferring personal violence: 1995 Act, s.5(3).

It may be competent to impose an even longer period of imprisonment and there are two sets of circumstances in which this is so. First, a statute might make provision for a longer period as with assaults on police constables: see Police (Scotland) Act 1967, s.41(1). Secondly, where an accused who having been granted bail fails to appear in court later or fails to comply with conditions of bail he or she may, if the failure amounts to a subsequent offence, competently be sentenced to an enhanced period of imprisonment: see the 1995 Act, s.27(5).

The summary powers of sheriffs are delineated by their territorial jurisdiction: 1995 Act, s.4(1). Each full-time sheriff is appointed to sit in a particular sheriffdom and where an offence is alleged to have been committed in one district in a sheriffdom it is competent to try that offence in a sheriff court in any other district in that sheriffdom: 1995 Act, s.4(2).

District court

Two points need to be noted at the outset: "courts of summary criminal jurisdiction" includes the sheriff court and district court: 1995 Act, s.307(1). If, however, a statute speaks of an offence being punishable "on summary conviction" or does not name the court, jurisdiction is conferred only on the sheriff court: *McPherson v Boyd* (1907).

Each area of a local authority is the district of a district court. The jurisdiction and powers of a district court are exercisable by a stipendiary magistrate or by one or more justices. All prosecutions in a commission area or local authority area proceed at the instance of the procurator fiscal: see generally the 1995 Act, ss. 6, 7 and 8.

A district court consists of a stipendiary magistrate (in Glasgow) or one or more justices of the peace and has criminal jurisdiction extending over the area having a distinct commission of the peace for which the justices are appointed.

A stipendiary magistrate has the summary criminal jurisdiction and powers of a sheriff: 1995 Act, s.7(5). That, in practice, means that a stipendiary magistrate has the power to imprison for a period not exceeding three months, although that power is enhanced by reason of previous dishonesty or personal violence. A district court constituted by a justice of the peace has a maximum competent power of imprisonment of 60 days and a fine not exceeding £2,500: 1995 Act, s.7(6) and (7).

As the powers of punishment are limited, the business before the district courts may reasonably be measured by volume rather than seriousness. An appeal against conviction and/or sentence under summary procedure is competent to the High Court of Justiciary.

Drugs courts

The general object of Drugs Courts is to combine close supervision by the judicial process with appropriate resources and support services. The prospect of a meaningless judicial sentence is used to motivate an individual to complete treatment. Drugs courts have been established in the Sheriff Courts in Glasgow and Kirkcaldy; Criminal Justice (Scotland) Act 2002, s.36. The powers of these courts include drug treatment and testing orders: Criminal Procedure (Scotland) Act 1995, ss.234B to 233K.

---

4. THE PERSONNEL

The Scottish legal system consists of a variety of offices and appointments. Some of these are of great antiquity and their origins are to be found in the early history of Scotland. Not all of the offices and appointments are held by lawyers.

THE LEGAL PROFESSION: LEGAL QUALIFICATIONS

Advocate

The Faculty of Advocates is the traditional Scottish Bar and members of the Faculty have a function and tradition which corresponds broadly to that of barristers in England and Wales, Northern Ireland and the Republic of Ireland.

The history of the Faculty is a very long one for it dates from the early sixteenth century and originates from a group of pleaders who regularly appeared before the courts preceding the Court of Session.

The principal officer of the Faculty is the Dean who takes precedence over all members of the Bar except the Lord Advocate in office. There is a Vice-Dean and other office bearers, all being elected annually at the anniversary meeting of the Faculty held in January each year. Office bearers tend to be re-elected while they are willing to serve.

Admission to the Faculty is by election after the intrant (the name for someone who intends to join) has petitioned the court, paid certain fees and satisfied the Faculty examiners as to his or her qualifications.

The affairs of the Faculty and the interests of the members are managed by an elected Council. The Dean acting through Discipline Panels and an Investigating Committee exercises control over the professional discipline and ethics of the members of the Faculty. There exist powers to censure or disbar a member who has acted in a manner amounting to professional or other serious misconduct, *e.g.* 1968 S.L.T. (News) 47 and *Lee v H.M. Advocate* (1968).

Solicitor

The lawyers now known as solicitors were previously designated writers or law agents and there still exist many small professional groups of considerable age. The principal of these are the Society of Writers to the Signet (1594), the Society of Solicitors in the Supreme Courts (1797), the Royal Faculty of Procurators in Glasgow (1796) and the Society of Advocates in Aberdeen (1774). The last named is indeed a society of solicitors and is not to be confused with the Faculty of Advocates.

There was some legislation in the early part of this century but the establishment of the Law Society in Scotland in 1949 was a major watershed. The role of Registrar of Solicitors and the issuing of various rules as to professional practice, conduct and discipline have centralised the position of the Law Society of Scotland in regard to solicitors.

Admission to the Roll of Solicitors, a roll maintained by the Registrar, is by petition following the attainment of a law degree at a Scottish university, or the passing of professional examinations in place of such a degree. There is also a requirement to obtain a Diploma in Legal Practice at a Scottish university and a period of training with a practising solicitor. A solicitor in practice must take out a practising certificate annually: see generally the Solicitors (Scotland) Act 1980 and associated delegated legislation.

Solicitor advocate

Until 1993, solicitors were not entitled to plead before the superior courts, although they tended to be intimately involved in the preparation of cases and often sat beside the advocate who did present the case.

In an attack on various monopolistic powers the Government made provision for solicitors to obtain extended rights of audience, either in the High Court of Justiciary or, alternatively, the civil courts constituting the Court of Session, the House of Lords and the Judicial Committee of the Privy Council.

Solicitors with at least five years' continuous experience of court work may apply for either extended criminal rights of audience or such civil rights, or both. After some further training and an examination such solicitors attain extended rights of audience.

Notaries public

The office of notary public is ancient and in legal systems elsewhere is sometimes a separate office. In Scotland changes in 1896 meant that only enrolled solicitors were admitted to the role of notaries public. The function of notaries is essentially to authenticate formal deeds, especially where such documents are intended for use abroad.

THE LEGAL PROFESSION: ROLES

Counsel

Advocates, also known as junior counsel, have regard to the date of call to the Bar to determine seniority. Junior counsel remain junior until advanced to the rank and dignity of Queen's Counsel, otherwise known as senior counsel.

Senior counsel are generally appointed after a number of years' experience in practice, or in Parliament or in teaching law at a university. Appointment is by the Queen, on the recommendation of the Lord Justice-General.

Amongst themselves Queen's Counsel take precedence according to the dates of their respective letters patent (the royal letter of appointment), except that the Lord Advocate in office has precedence over all others. At the installation of a judge, for example, the order of precedence ensures that the Lord Advocate is entitled to seat "within the Bar", that is, in the well of the court, at the clerk's table on the right side of the clerk. The Dean of Faculty ranks next in precedence and has a seat at the centre of the Bar. The Solicitor General for Scotland in office ranks third and has a seat within the Bar at the clerk's table on the left side of the clerk.

In litigation Queen's Counsel wears a silk gown and he or she may lead any other counsel not of that rank, whatever the date of call to the Bar of junior counsel. When in court counsel invariably wears a wig, usually the short bob wig but on more formal occasions the full wig. Primarily, counsel represents a party in proceedings before any court or tribunal. As well as such appearance before courts and tribunals, counsel will normally have been involved in the earlier stages of the case and in advising about it.

In criminal cases, counsel will consider precognitions and take instructions on matters such as special defences as well as offering advice on what plea ought to be stated. In civil cases, counsel may advise on whether to bring a claim, in which court, and for what remedy or, alternatively, whether to defend. Counsel is not restricted to oral advice and, indeed, may be instructed primarily to draft and revise all necessary court documents.

It is an error to link counsel invariably with litigation. Counsel is frequently consulted on matters not necessarily the subject of litigation. An opinion on a point of law or on the quantification of a claim may be accepted as a basis for settlement. The legal problem, or matter in issue, is set down in a Memorial with any documents with specific questions for counsel on which answers are sought. The answers are returned in the form of a written opinion after the necessary legal research has been undertaken.

It is only to be expected that some counsel specialise in particular areas of the law, and the opinions of counsel are frequently sought on the basis of that expertise or because of the reputation of particular counsel. Either way, each counsel is alone personally and solely responsible for the opinions produced or documents drafted.

A legal relationship with another advocate or any other person for the purpose of jointly offering professional services is now permissible: Law Reform (Miscellaneous Provisions) (Scotland) Act 1990, s.31.

In the conduct of litigation senior and junior counsel are frequently instructed to appear in the same case and for the same side, that is, for the same client. Junior counsel carries out the drafting and adjusting of written pleadings and related matters. Depending on the seriousness of the case and the experience of those involved, senior and junior counsel may consult as the work proceeds.

At a hearing in court senior counsel normally conducts the examination and cross-examination of the witnesses, or at least the most important and difficult witnesses, while junior counsel assists by noting evidence and assisting generally. There are, however, no predetermined rules and counsel appearing together regularly can reach their own agreement on the division of labour.

A client may normally instruct counsel only through an enrolled solicitor. At meetings with counsel the client is accompanied by the solicitor. The choice of counsel is determined by the nature of the case and the expertise of counsel as well as the knowledge of the solicitor of other matters, such as the likely preference of the client.

Instructions come to counsel from a solicitor but exceptionally an advocate may accept instructions from persons who are not solicitors, for example, chartered accountants, chartered surveyors, patent agents, parliamentary agents or lawyers outwith Scotland in matters in which no litigation in Scotland is contemplated or in progress: see [1970] C.L.Y. 3405.

Once an advocate has accepted instructions in a civil matter to act in a case, he or she must remain free to act according to his or her judgment and discretion: *Batchelor v Pattison and Mackersy* (1876). Counsel may thus take a particular course of action or even abandon or compromise a claim on his or her own responsibility: *Mackintosh v Fraser* (1860). Such an approach, however, could not be adopted if there had been a clear instruction not to do so.

There has been a famous assertion of the essence of the task of the advocate:

"The nature of an advocate's office makes it clear that in performance of his duty he must be entirely independent and act according to his own discretion and judgment in the conduct of the cause of his client. His legal right is to conduct the case without any regard to the wishes of his client, so long as his mandate is unrecalled, and what he does bona fide according to his own judgment will bind his client and will not expose him to any action for what he has done, even if his client's interests are thereby predecided": *Batchelor v Pattison and Mackersy* (1876) at 918.

In criminal matters, an accused has a right to a fair trial. However, the accused's legal representative is not subject to the accused's direction as to how the defence is to be presented, although that representative has to act according to his or her instructions as to what the defence is and cannot disregard them: *Anderson v H.M. Advocate* (1996) at 163. The way in which the accused's legal representative conducts the defence within his instructions is a matter for him or her to decide and as a general rule the accused is bound by them: *Anderson v H.M. Advocate* (1996) at 165.

However, a client remains free at any time to withdraw an instruction to one counsel and thereafter to instruct another counsel to act in the place of the former. An advocate is not in general bound to disclose information obtained once instructed, unless the client waives the privilege.

On grounds of public policy and by custom an advocate may not be liable in damages for wrong advice in law, negligence, mistake, indiscretion, error of judgment or the mismanagement of a cause: *Batchelor v Pattison and Mackersy* (1876). There may be such liability by express agreement or if the advocate has acted fraudulently or treacherously: *Swinfern v Lord Chelmsford* (1860). A solicitor in an action is not liable who acts upon the advice of counsel familiar with that type of action in matters connected with the conduct of a cause: *Dixon v Rutherford* (1863).

Advocates tend to work at home or in the Advocates Library in Parliament House where each has a box for papers to be delivered to or uplifted. Complaints against advocates may be put to the Dean of Faculty, who has an office in the Advocates Library, and he has powers in relation to such relevant misconduct as may be admitted or proved.

Solicitors

The designation "solicitor" follows from the Solicitors (Scotland) Act 1933 but the terms "writer" and also "law agent" are still used. Many solicitors are employed by central and local government or by companies in industry and commerce.

However, the largest group of solicitors is that consisting of solicitors in private practice. As a consequence much of the law controlling or delimiting the role of solicitor is heavily influenced by the conditions of private practice.

The employment of a solicitor is regulated by the general principles of the law of agency; hence, perhaps, the old term of law agent. The extent of a solicitor's authority depends on the nature of the work he or she has been instructed to undertake.

A solicitor is entitled to a measure of discretion in the conduct of litigation although that discretion may be constrained by the directions of counsel where one has also been instructed: *Buchanan v Davidson* (1877).

A solicitor may not abandon a claim without authority from a client: *Thoms v Bain* (1888). The actings of a solicitor are binding on the client provided they do not go beyond what is necessary for achieving the end for which the solicitor was employed, or what is usual in the exercise of the authority conferred: *Sanderson v Campbell* (1833).

The nature of the work of a solicitor is so varied as to be difficult to categorise, especially as many stray from what may be the practice of law properly so-called to management or administration. Nevertheless, it can be said that the sale and purchase of land and buildings, winding up estates of deceased people, the administration of trusts, company work, and representation of clients before courts and tribunals, or the preparation for such representation, all feature prominently.

The extent to which the Law Society of Scotland seeks to regulate the members of that Society varies in regard to the nature of their work. Solicitors in private practice must comply with the Solicitors (Scotland) Accounts Rules and produce an accountant's certificate every six months that their accounts have been kept in accordance with the rules. Solicitors in employment are less closely constrained.

Solicitors undertake to perform business entrusted to them with due diligence and skill: *Bell v Ogilvie* (1863). They will be liable in damages for loss sustained by the client in consequence of breach of this duty: *Steward v Mclean, Baird and Neilson* (1915).

Professional negligence varies with circumstances but solicitors in private practice must be covered by insurance against such claims. A Scottish Solicitors' Guarantee Fund exists to compensate individuals who have sustained loss in consequence of a solicitor's dishonesty: Solicitors (Scotland) Act 1980, s.43.

A solicitor will not, however, be held liable in damages for giving incorrect advice on a doubtful point of law where there has been no clear rule or practice, as that is properly the function of counsel: *Blair v Assets Co* (1896). A solicitor will not be held liable if he follows the usual course of practice even if it should be held that that was incorrect: *Hamilton v Emslie* (1868). It is not professional misconduct to bring an action if that is advised by counsel: *X Insurance Co v A and B* (1936).

Advice on doubtful or difficult matters has generally been the province of counsel. Also, in the past, the proper course in such event was to put before counsel a Memorial with the relevant facts to obtain the opinion of counsel. Whether that remains the correct approach, given the high degree of specialism in the practice of some solicitors, is debatable.

In private practice, it is common for solicitors to form partnerships or to join partnerships that have subsisted over many years. The reasons for this are essentially commercial, although such arrangements assist with specialisation.

Until 1990 a solicitor was not entitled to form a partnership with a non-solicitor: 1980 Act, s.27. However, such partnerships are now permitted and there may now exist multi-disciplinary partnerships involving several professions: Law Reform (Miscellaneous Provisions) (Scotland) Act 1990, s.31(3).

It is competent for solicitors in Scotland to enter into multi-national practices with foreign lawyers registered as such with the Law Society of Scotland. It is equally competent for advocates or solicitors in Scotland who have obtained comparable qualifications in England or elsewhere to practice in other jurisdictions subject to compliance with the practice rules of the other jurisdictions. Equally, a European Community Directive of 1977 (77/249) required Members States to permit lawyers from another Member State to offer legal services within their jurisdictions. While such changes are entirely consistent with ensuring the free movement of services, the practical difficulties where lawyers have no knowledge or experience of Scots law are obvious.

Rights of audience

It will have been noted that lawyers do much else other than appear in court for clients. However, the courts are public *fora* and the efficient conduct and administration of litigation requires there to be certainty as to who may appear where. The rights of audience may conveniently be considered under two headings: non-lawyers and lawyers.

Non-lawyers
A party to a civil case brought before a court or tribunal may appear and present his or her own case personally. An accused in a criminal case may defend himself or herself and, in the absence of funds or legal aid, may be required to do so.
An individual, however, may not appear or speak for a spouse: *Gordon v Nakeski Cumming* (1924). An individual may not appear for a parent: *Rush v Fife R.C.* (1984). An individual may not appear for his or her employer: *Dana v Stevenson* (1989). An individual may not appear for a firm of which he is a partner: *Macbeth and Maclagan v Macmillan* (1914). An individual may not appear for a company of which he or she is a director: *Equity and Law Life Assurance Society v Tritonia Ltd* (1943). An individual may not appear for a club of which he is a treasurer: *Strathclyde R.C. v Sheriff Clerk (Glasgow)* (1992). A petitioner to the High Court of Justiciary may only present himself, and if he chooses not to do so only a legally qualified representative may appear: *Robbie The Pict v H.M. Advocate*, 2002 S.C.C.R. 213.
The right of audience is less restricted before the lower courts for some types of action. For example, in the sheriff court a party to proceedings under the Debtors (Scotland) Act 1987 is entitled, except in appeals to the sheriff principal, to be represented by a non-lawyer provided the sheriff is satisfied that the person is suitable and duly authorised: Sheriff Court Ordinary Cause Rules, rule 2.
A Reporter to the Children's Panel with at least one year's experience is entitled to conduct proceedings, under the relevant parts of the Children (Scotland) Act 1995: SI 1997/714 as amended by SI 1997/1084. There is some doubt as to whether the right of audience extends to appeals to the sheriff principal. Although the explanatory note to the regulations states that proceedings before the sheriff includes those before the sheriff principal, this proposition has been doubted: *Templeton v E* (1998).
The right of audience is least restricted before tribunals. Any person may appear before an industrial tribunal in person to be represented by counsel or solicitor or by a representative of a trade union or an employer's association or by any other person whom he desires to represent him or her: Employment Protection Consolidation Act 1978, Sch.9, para.6.
This right to appear before a tribunal is not dependent on any preliminary qualification or training. However, any professional or other body, for the purpose of enabling any of their members who is a natural person to acquire rights to conduct litigation on behalf of members of the public and rights of audience, may make an application to the Lord President and the Secretary of State with a draft scheme specifying the courts, categories of proceedings, nature of business and rights of litigation and representation sought, and giving certain other information: Law Reform (Miscellaneous Provisions) (Scotland) Act 1990, ss.25 to 29.

Lawyers

Advocates have rights of audience before the European Court, the House of Lords, Judicial Committee of the Privy Council, various parliamentary committees, the Court of Session, the High Court of Justiciary, the sheriff and district courts and all inferior courts and tribunals, inquiries and other hearings unless they are excluded by express rule of law.

Solicitors have right of audience in the European Court, the sheriff and district courts and all tribunals, inquiries and other hearings unless they are excluded by express rule of law.

All solicitors have a right of audience before a vacation judge: Court of Session Act 1988, s.48(2). Solicitors may also obtain a right of audience in the supreme courts in such circumstances as may be prescribed: Law Reform (Miscellaneous Provisions) (Scotland) Act 1990, Sch.8, para.38. Finally, in all proceedings before an appeal judge, and in all preliminary and interlocutory proceedings and applications except such as are heard before the full court, the parties may be represented and appear by a solicitor alone: Criminal Procedure (Scotland) Act 1995, s.103(5) and (8). Solicitors with extended rights of audience in terms of the 1990 Act, s.24 are entitled to appear in the appropriate court.

Legal officials

Judges

Two places among the Lords of Appeal in Ordinary are usually filled by Scots-qualified lawyers. Additionally a number of Scots who are English-qualified have held these appointments. The vacancies are filled by the Queen appointing on the advice of the Prime Minister. Those so appointed have been the Lord President, Court of Session Lords Ordinary from the Inner or Outer House, or those appointed directly from the Bar. The retirement age is 75 years.

The appointment as a Lord Ordinary of the Court of Session and the Lord Commissioner of Justiciary is made by the Queen on the nomination of the Secretary of State for Scotland who consults the Lord Advocate. The Lord Advocate may propose, and frequently has in the past, himself for promotion to the Bench.

Apart from the Lord Advocate, those available for selection hitherto have been at the practising Bar, usually a Law Officer, former Home Advocate Depute or a senior member of the Faculty of Advocates.

The group eligible now extends to sheriffs principal and sheriffs who have held office for five years, and advocates and solicitors who have had for at least five years rights of audience in both the Court of Session and the High Court of Justiciary: Law Reform (Miscellaneous Provisions) (Scotland) Act 1990, Sch.4, para.1. Whatever the route of appointment the retiring age is 70 years.

Sheriffs

A sheriff principal is appointed from Queens Counsel or advocates or solicitors or sheriffs of at least 10 years' standing. A sheriff is similarly appointed from Queens Counsel, advocates or solicitors of at least ten years' standing. A sheriff may resign office and resume practice. Retirement of full-time sheriffs principal and sheriffs on pension is compulsory at 70 years.

Stipendiary magistrates and justices of the peace

Stipendiary magistrates are appointed by a local authority from among qualified legal practitioners. Justices of the Peace are partly appointed by local councils, which may nominate one quarter of their members as justices; the remainder are appointed by the Secretary of State for Scotland on the recommendation of local committees which try to secure that justices are broadly representative of the local community. There are no particular qualifications for appointment: District Courts (Scotland) Act 1975, ss.5 and 9.

Law officers

The Crown has two traditional official advisers or Law Officers, the Lord Advocate and the Solicitor General for Scotland. They are appointed by the Prime Minister and go out of office with the Government. Either or both may be Members of Parliament, although in practice it is less common for both to be so. If the Lord Advocate is not a Member of the House of Commons on appointment then he is traditionally made a Member of the House of Lords by being created a life peer.

The Law Officers assist with the handling of Government business and they advise the Crown and represent it in civil cases. The Lord Advocate is the supreme public prosecutor in the criminal courts and has complete discretion in the prosecution of crimes. The Law Officers appear in court from time to time, usually, though not necessarily, in the more serious cases.

In the Scottish Parliament there is a Scottish Executive comprising the First Minister, such other ministers as may be appointed and both the Lord Advocate and the Solicitor General: the Scotland Act 1998, s.44(1). If the Lord Advocate or the Solicitor General are not members of the Scottish Parliament they may be allowed to participate in the proceedings but they may not vote: s.27(1).

The creation of the Scottish Parliament has resulted in a third Law Officer, namely the Advocate General, whose concern in essence is providing advice to the United Kingdom Government on matters of Scots law and the constitutional or legal propriety of the Scottish Parliament in the context of its powers. The Scotland Act 1998 provides, in Sch.6, for "devolution issues" which amount to questions about Bills being within the legal competency of the Scottish Parliament or about other functions of the Scottish Executive. Where such questions arise the Advocate

General may prevent a Bill being sent for Royal Assent and refer the matter to the Judicial Committee of the Privy Council: ss.32 and 33.

Advocates-depute

The Lord Advocate appoints a number of Advocates-Depute to assist him in the prosecution of criminal cases in the High Court of Justiciary. The senior of these deputes is the Home Depute who has a supervisory role and tends to deal with Edinburgh cases. The Home Depute is a senior member of the Bar and some of the other Advocates-Depute may also be such. Since time immemorial Advocates-Depute have been advocates, but one solicitor has been appointed full time and several on an ad hoc basis in recent years. The duties of Advocates-Depute now are very extensive and those at the Bar can barely maintain a civil practice while holding down what is supposed to be a part-time appointment.

Standing junior counsel

A wide variety of United Kingdom Government departments and boards and many exclusively Scottish departments have standing junior counsel. They act as legal advisers to and counsel for these offices. Holders of these posts do so while also maintaining a legal practice. Standing junior counsel resign office when taking silk.

The Lord Advocate's department

This small department assists the Law Officers. The lawyers within the office are known as legal secretaries and they also act as parliamentary draftsmen. They deal with exclusively Scottish matters and advise on the Scottish interests arising out of UK measures.

Crown Agent

The Crown Agent is the permanent head of the Crown Office in Edinburgh and he is the senior civil servant charged with management of the Procurator Fiscal Service. The Crown Agent is not to be thought of as the Lord Advocate's instructing solicitor because the discretion inherent in the duties of the Lord Advocate is not amenable to such instruction. The Crown Agent in the modern era has tended to have had experience as a procurator fiscal prior to that appointment.

The Reporter

Each local authority area has a Children's Panel with panel members appointed by the Scottish Ministers with local advice. A hearing takes place to deal with matters referred to it by the Reporter. The Reporter is the initiator of proceedings (even though these proceedings are in no sense to be equated with a prosecution) and the Reporter acts in effect as clerk and legal adviser to the tribunal. The panel may impose compulsory measures of supervision on a child in certain conditions, for example where a child is beyond control of any relevant person: Children (Scotland) Act 1995, s.52(2)(a). There can be referrals to the sheriff court. The Reporter is not to be seen as a prosecutor as the paramount consideration throughout is the welfare of the child throughout his or her childhood: 1995 Act, s.16(1).

The Queen's and Lord Treasurer's Remembrancer

In 1981 the Crown Agent was appointed simultaneously to be the Queen's and Lord Treasurer's Remembrancer. The Remembrancer is the Treasury representative in Scotland and the Accounting Officer for the Vote for Law Charges and Courts of Law, Scotland. The officer makes payments from the Consolidated Fund of legal salaries and from the various Votes of Parliament administered by the Scottish departments. Many of the remaining duties are of a similar accounting nature.

Solicitor to the Secretary of State for Scotland

The Solicitor's Office acts in legal matters for all the departments of Scottish Office and for other United Kingdom departments such as Treasury which have functions in Scotland. As well as general legal advice the legal staff also conduct conveyancing and reparation work and deal with tribunal and other court work.

The Accountant of Court

This officer of the Court of Session is appointed by the Secretary of State on the nomination of the Lord Advocate. The Accountant of Court supervises the conduct of persons judicially appointed by the Court of Session or sheriff court to be a judicial factor or curator bonis to administer the estates of persons incapable of doing so themselves, and annually audits and reports on their accounts and fixes their remuneration. Duties also include the supervision of those appointed trustees on sequestrated estates.

The Accountant in Bankruptcy

This accountant has the function of supervising interim trustees, permanent trustees in bankruptcy and commissioners and maintaining registers of bankruptcies, trust deeds and similar matters. Trustees are required to report to the Accountant in Bankruptcy to seek authority for certain procedures: see Bankruptcy (Scotland) Act 1985.

The police

The police in Scotland are not a national force but separate forces administered by local councils as police authorities: Police (Scotland) Act 1967 as amended and supplemented by much other legislation. There are other police forces with particular jurisdictions, such as defence establishments: for example, Ministry of Defence Police Act 1987. The general function of the police is to preserve law and order: the 1967 Act, s.17. The police are required to report detected crime to procurators fiscal for consideration for prosecution, and the police do not decide upon prosecutions and do not prosecute in any court. The efficiency of the individual forces is assessed and reported on by Her Majesty's Inspector of Constabulary.

The prison service

The Scottish Office Home and Health Department, acting through the Scottish Prison Board, administers prisons, borstals and similar penal institutions in Scotland. There is a Chief Inspector of Prisons and an Ombudsman to visit prisons and hear complaints.

Keeper of the Registers of Scotland

The Keeper is appointed by the Secretary of State with the consent of the Lord President and is Head of the Executive Agency of the Registers of Scotland. The Agency maintains 16 separate registers and the registration of many deeds and documents relating to legal matters. The single most important of these is the General Register of Sasines in which are registered writs relating to rights in land.

Registrar General

The Registrar General of Births, Deaths and Marriages for Scotland, acting through a network of district registrars, registers births, deaths, marriages, adoptions and related events and collects statistical information.

---

5. LEGISLATION AND PRECEDENT

The major formal sources of law can be said to be legislation and precedent. Legislation includes Acts of Parliament as well as legislation by delegates of Parliament, and European Union legislation. Precedent is essentially the rules produced and applied by courts with reference to Parliament or any other legislature. Each of these sources may be considered separately.

EUROPEAN LEGISLATION

The European Union is supra-national, somewhat similar to a federation (such as the United States of America) and also similar to an international organisation (such as the United Nations). The institutions are the European Commission, the E.G. Council, the European Parliament and the European Court of Justice. Attached to the last is a Court of First Instance. There is also a body known as the Committee of Permanent Representatives (COREPER—the French acronym for the Committee of Permanent Representatives) which is responsible for preparing the work of the E.G. Council.

There are five sources of European law. First, the founding treaties, accession treaties providing for the accession of new member states, ancillary protocols and conventions, treaties amplifying or amending the founding treaties, conventions between Member States concluded within the ambit of the founding treaties, such as the Convention on Jurisdiction and the Enforcement of Judgments in Civil and Commercial Matters of 1968, agreements with non-member states of associations of such states, and other international agreements.

Secondly, there are regulations and directives as well as decisions of European Union institutions.

Thirdly, there is case law of the European Court of Justice.

Fourthly, there are general principles from the constitutions and legal systems of Member States or international agreements to which the Member States are parties.

Finally, there are influential reports, answers to questions asked in the European Parliament and statements issued by the Commission.

The authority to make legislation for the European Union, and the method of making legislation, must be found in the treaties. Some articles of the treaties give specific powers to the Council of Ministers to legislate. Other articles impose obligations without expressly giving the power to legislate. There is a separate power to enable the Council of Ministers, acting according to a certain procedure, to legislate to attain objectives of the European Union.

The basic legislative procedure involves the Council of Ministers approving a proposal and then passing it to the European Parliament. That forum then remits the proposal to one of its committees for a report, which may contain suggested amendments, upon which Parliament votes. Members of the Commission may appear in order to explain the proposal. The view of Parliament is sent back to the Council of Ministers, which passes them on to one of its working groups, co-ordinated by COREPER. This group comprises national civil servants, who examine it in the light of individual national interests.

If a mutually acceptable version is produced it is accepted by the Council of Ministers. If such a version is not, then the Council of Ministers seek a compromise which is voted on, or referred back to COREPER. The powers of the European Parliament are, comparatively speaking, not great. There is, however, a "co-operation procedure", which increases the power of the European Parliament to amend proposals. After the existing consultation procedure with the European Parliament, the Council produces a common position. The Parliament may (by an absolute majority) accept this; it may reject it, in which case it can be adopted only by a unanimous vote of the Council; or it may (by an absolute majority) seek amendment which the Council (by a qualified majority) may accept or reject.

There has also been an increase in the power of the European Parliament through a "co-decision procedure". The proposal of the Commission, after initial consultation, is submitted to the Council and European Parliament simultaneously. If the Parliament (by an absolute majority) rejects it, the Council may convene a Conciliation Committee of equal numbers of representatives of Council and Parliament, assisted by the Commission, with a view to agreeing within six weeks a text acceptable to the Council (by a qualified majority) and to Parliament (by an absolute majority). If it fails, the proposal falls unless the Council adopts its original position, or as amended by the Parliament, within a further six weeks. Parliament, nevertheless, by an absolute majority may veto this within six months.

Enforcement of European legislation

An enforcement action may be brought by the European Commission against a Member State appearing not to be fulfilling its community obligations, and such an action is heard in the European Court of Justice. The court may also hear a preliminary reference from a national court or tribunal with a view to ensuring consistent decisions on validity and interpretation throughout the Union.

In application of European Union legislation two principles are paramount. First, European law is intended to supersede national law where the two conflict, and this is the principle of primacy. Secondly, European law is intended to have direct effect, and this means that enforcement actions may be brought in court where such legislation had the intention of direct applicability. Generally, regulations have general application and are directly applicable without the need for confirmation or other action by national legislatures. Directives are binding as to the result to be achieved but they have to be implemented by the national legislatures in whatever manner they deem appropriate.

Direct effect is divided into "vertical" and "horizontal". European Union law may place an obligation with direct effect upon a Member State. If it does so and the obligation is not fulfilled, those suffering consequential loss may sue the Member State. This proceeds on the basis that the Member State is next up in the hierarchy above the aggrieved party and it is described as vertical direct effect: see, *e.g. Van Gend en Loos* (1963).

Alternatively, European Union law may place an obligation with direct effect upon a person or company. If it does so and the obligation is not fulfilled, those suffering consequential loss may sue the person or company. This proceeds on the basis that the person or company are on the same level and it is described as horizontal direct effect: see, *e.g. Defrenne v Sabena* (1976).

There are two conditions necessary to create direct effect. First, the legislation must be clearly and specifically enough drafted for a court to be able to apply it. Secondly, it must create an unqualified right or duty and it must not require action by some other body before a court can apply it.

European legislation and United Kingdom law

The European Communities Act 1972 ensured the applicability of European law in the United Kingdom, and section 2(1) provides that all directly effective Community legislation (already made or to be made, and whether as treaty, regulation, directive or decision) creates "enforceable community right"); that is, it has direct effect in the United Kingdom, and will be enforced by courts and tribunals, and United Kingdom law is to be applied subject to it.

Moreover, that section is supported by s.3(1) and (2). These provide that judges are to be presumed to know the content and significance of the treaties, the content of the Official Journal of the European Communities and of decisions of the European Court of Justice. Further, these provisions establish that questions of the validity and interpretation of community law, if not actually sent to the European Court of Justice for a preliminary reference, must be decided in accordance with the decisions of the court and the principles laid down there.

The revolutionary nature of these principles lies in their undermining the previous concept of parliamentary supremacy. The implications of the sections of the 1972 Act cited above were at their clearest in *R. v Secretary of State for Transport, ex parte Factortame (No. 2)* (1990). Two preliminary references and an appeal to the House of Lords established that an Act of Parliament contradicting, and passed after, certain European Union legislation, could not be enforced in the courts of the United Kingdom. Further, because European Union law had to be enforced, courts were entitled to issue orders carrying it out, even though national law gave no such right.

The preliminary references follow from an obligation to refer questions of the validity or interpretation of European Union law to the European Court of Justice. These references—known as Art.177 references—are usually discretionary although there is no authority as to when such a reference is appropriate. It has been suggested by the House of Lords that there should be such a reference when a novel point of law arose, or where there is no constant series of decisions from the European Court of Justice: *Garland v B.R. Engineering Ltd* (1982). For Scottish examples see *Walkingshaw v Marshall* (1992) and *Westwater v Thomson* (1992).

UK PARLIAMENTARY LEGISLATION

Introduction

Parliamentary legislation tends generally speaking to be initiated by the Government. The legislation is, accordingly, often directed to change society or some part of it to meet the policy of the particular Government. Not all such legislation has that sole purpose for some legislation may simply be routine or expedient irrespective of the aims of the Government of the day.

The majority of statutes from Parliament are public general statutes. The number varies each year, and so too does the length of the Act. For example, the Income and Corporation Taxes Act 1988 has nearly 1,500 sections in order to codify tax law. The Criminal Procedure (Intermediate Diets) (Scotland) Act 1988 had only a couple of sections to clarify a small but important point of procedure.

The conventional structure of a modern statute requires a short title, a chapter number and also a long title and a preamble. The enacting formula is followed with headings and relevant sections, including an interpretation section.

The consequences of the Act require, possibly, repeals, amendments and transitional provisions, along with commencement provisions and provisions dealing with the extent of application. Many modern Acts have Schedules, which are now incorporated into the Act by a section, and these Schedules contain detailed provisions to provide for the consequences of the legislative change.

Parliamentary stages

The procedures and privileges of the United Kingdom Parliament are conveniently set out in a single volume, but they are extensive and detailed: that volume, often known as "the parliamentary Bible", is Erskine May's *Treatise on the Law, Privileges, Proceedings and Usage of Parliament* (C.J. Boulton, 21st ed., 1989).

A Bill may be introduced into either of the Houses of Parliament in London by any Member of Parliament or peer. In practice most Bills are Government Bills and are therefore introduced by a member of the Government. Further, the majority of Government Bills, and certainly controversial or taxation and expenditure Bills, are introduced into the House of Commons first.

The first reading of the Bill is its introduction and this stage is purely formal. It may be, however, that this becomes the first sight that the public has of a controversial Bill. The second reading follows after time for consideration of the detail. There is then a debate on the general principles behind the Bill.

The second reading is the substantive stage at which the Bill can be debated, both on its principles and its details, on the floor of the House, and if there is a vote then the Government should win on a Government Bill because of its majority in the House of Commons. The peers in the House of Lords tend not to vote against legislation which has been supported by a majority in the House of Commons, but there have been exceptions.

The committee stage is the point at which the detail of the Bill is examined closely to try to assess if it achieves its purpose. Amendments are proposed and considered by the committee.

The nature of the duties of committees requires more time than would be possible and available on the floor of either House. The speed of the work of the committee depends on the extent to which there is opposition to the purpose of the Bill. Membership of these committees reflects the political balance in the House of Commons, and a Committee of the Whole House in the House of Lords. Moreover, in many Bills the attention of committees is directed to controversial clauses and many other dependent or peripheral clauses go by without scrutiny.

The report stage is when the relevant committee reports its amendments to the Whole House. Amendments may still be proposed at this stage.

The third reading is when the House may consider and give approval to the final formulation of the Bill. This need not be at the end of procedure as Bills may be commenced in either House, and that makes it necessary to allow the first House to consider and give approval to any amendments of the second House. The procedural path of a Bill ends with royal assent, which on past form is essentially formal, but it does make a Bill an Act.

Special legislation

There are a number of special cases of legislation. First, financial legislation is required annually as a control on the executive. Thus, annual Finance Acts permit taxation and the Consolidated Fund and Appropriation Acts permit Government expenditure.

Secondly, there is constitutional legislation under the Parliament Acts 1911 and 1949. These statutes affect the House of Lords in various ways: (i) Bills certified by the speaker as "money Bills" (such as taxation and expenditure Bills) can be delayed by the House of Lords for one month, after which they are deemed to have agreed to them; (ii) other bills (unless they fall into the third category) can be delayed for two sessions of Parliament, after which they are deemed to be agreed; and (iii) Bills to extend the life of Parliament and any private legislation are unaffected by the legislation referred to.

Thirdly, major revision and repeal of statute law is undertaken from time to time. The two Law Commissions have responsibility for that task and the legislation governing such revision and repeal has resulted in an abbreviated procedure.

Fourthly, consolidating statutes result in related provisions in different Acts being placed in a single Act. Such a proposition is easier to state than to undertake because of the great complexity of many of the related provisions and because the subject matter of the Acts moves on requiring further consolidation. This parliamentary activity also follows an abbreviated procedure.

Fifthly, there is local, personal, private and hybrid legislation. The Private Bill procedure is used for legislation promoted by private individuals outwith Parliament, such as local authorities, who petition Parliament for legislation. This procedure involves a quasi-judicial procedure in which promoters and objectors give evidence. A private Act will always be "local" or "personal".

Private legislation is now very rare because local authorities have certain powers under public general legislation that avoids the necessity of such legislation: see *e.g.* the Local Government (Scotland) Act 1973, s.203. The path of personal private legislation has now been smoothed with an accelerated procedure.

Hybrid legislation is that which is partly public interest and partly private local (or personal). There is a modified public Bill procedure.

An important evidential point should be noted here: the Interpretation Act 1978, s.3 stipulates that every Act is a public Act unless the Act states otherwise. When an Act is cited in court it does not require to be proved as such but is presumed to be law because it is a public Act.

Private legislation is entirely different from private members' legislation. Individual Members of Parliament or peers may introduce, or try to introduce, legislation. Private members may introduce Bills by two methods. First, the "10 minute rule" allows a private member on certain occasions to introduce a Bill and speak in favour of it for 10 minutes, after which another member can oppose it, also for 10 minutes, and then a vote is taken. Few members succeed under this rule.

Secondly, participating members may enter a ballot and if their name is selected earliest they are likely to receive time but little other support, and actual Government opposition if the subject of the private member's Bill is inconsistent with Government policy.

SCOTTISH PARLIAMENTARY LEGISLATION

Detailed provisions are included in the Scotland Act to ensure that each Bill proposed is subjected to scrutiny to prevent the creeping in of any provision that is beyond the powers of the Scottish Parliament. For example, on or before the introduction of a Bill into the Parliament, the member of the Scottish Executive in charge of it must make a statement that the provisions of the Bill are within the legislative competence of the Parliament. The Presiding Officer must also consider the matter and make a statement to Parliament as to whether or not the proposal is within that legislative competence.

The arrangements made for the passing of Bills in the Scottish Parliament are designed to simplify the process considerably compared to Westminster. The Scotland Act 1998 by s.3 establishes that a Bill should normally have the following stages: (1) a general debate on a Bill; and (2) consideration by Members of the Scottish Parliament of the details of the Bill; and (3) a final stage at which can be passed or rejected. Consultation on Bills at all stages is vital as the Scottish Parliament has no second chamber to revise a Bill. There are now established stages.

Stage 1

First, after introduction the relevant committee considers the general principles of the Bill, taking account of the views, if any, of other committees, and it also considers the Scottish Parliament's policy memorandum. Second, the full Parliament considers the general principles of the Bill in the context of the report. The Scottish Parliament then decides, on a vote if necessary, whether or not the general principles of the Bill are agreed to. If they are agreed then the Bill proceeds to Stage 2, but if not the Bill fails. This stage is equivalent to the second reading in the United Kingdom Parliament.

Stage 2

After a period of at least two weeks between the completion of Stage 1 and the commencement of Stage 2, the Bill is referred back to the relevant committee. The committee then examines each section of the Bill ("section" being the correct term rather than "clause" as in a United Kingdom Bill). Any MSP may move an amendment, but an MSP who is not a member of the relevant committee may not vote on an amendment.

Stage 3

Again, a period of at least two weeks must lapse between the completion of Stage 2 and the commencement of Stage 3. As this stage is taken by the full Parliament, every MSP has one opportunity to consider the Bill in its amended form. Stage 3 is the equivalent of the report and third reading in the United Kingdom Parliament. After a short delay a Bill may then be presented to the Queen by the Presiding Officer for royal assent.

DELEGATED LEGISLATION

Delegated legislation is sometimes known as subordinate or secondary legislation. The purpose of this legislation is to amplify parliamentary legislation, to provide for matters of detail, to bring particular provisions into force, and to give effect in particular matters to the general purpose and policy of an Act.

Legislation that is delegated is not to be thought of as a lesser form of legislation because, for example, it can be the means by which an Act of Parliament is actually brought into force, or it can be used to vary the criminal law by classifying a substance as a controlled drug or declassifying such a substance. Such delegated legislation is now very common and very voluminous. The majority of the items of delegated legislation are required to be registered, numbered and published: see the Statutory Instruments Act 1946.

Delegated legislation, if validly made and within the powers of the delegating Act, has the same force and effect as if it were contained in the principal Act itself. Statutory instruments do not require to be proved: *Macmillan v McConnell* (1917). There are now thousands of individual examples of delegated legislation.

There are a number of types or forms of subordinate legislation and the principal Acts are as follows:

(1) Orders in Council. Some Orders in Council are issued by the Queen in Council in exercise of the prerogative power. Parliament may also by statute authorise Her Majesty in Council to make Orders in Council.

(2) Orders of Council. Statutes, such as the Medical Act 1978, s.27, authorise the Privy Council to make orders for specified purposes. The authority is for the Privy Council and not the Queen and is often for the regulation of professional bodies and their disciplinary procedures.

(3) Rules, orders and instruments. Since 1947 the power conferred on a Minister or Department is now exercisable by statutory instrument, rather than the older name of rule or order: see generally the Statutory Instruments Act 1946. Although subject to parliamentary scrutiny, statutory instruments may relate to any topic at all if properly authorised.

(4) Local authority byelaws. The Local Government (Scotland) Act 1973, s.201 gives a general power to local authorities to make byelaws for the good rule and government of the council's area of authority. A municipal byelaw has been identified judicially as "an ordinance affecting the public or some portion of the public imposed by some authority clothed with statutory powers ordering something to be done or not to be done and accompanied by some sanction or penalty for its non-observance. Further, it involves this consequence, that if validly made it has the force of law within the sphere of its legitimate operation": *Kruse v Johnson* (1898) at 94.

(5) Acts of Sederunt and Acts of Adjournal. Judicial procedure is regulated by rules made under the inherent powers of the various courts

and under statute. The practical importance of these rules is great because of the need to comply with them in litigation. Acts of Sederunt regulate the Court of Session and the sheriff court: see Administration of Justice (Scotland) Act 1933, s.18. Acts of Adjournal regulate the High Court of Justiciary: see Criminal Procedure (Scotland) Act 1995, s.305.

STATUTORY INTERPRETATION

To construe or interpret a statute is a process of seeking to discover what the meaning and effect is to be given to that statute. It is not merely a theoretical task for it is usually undertaken in the context of a set of facts and circumstances. The process does arise in court cases but privately advice may be sought to discover the meaning of statutory provisions. Such interpretation may be necessary because words in statutes may be ambiguous in that the words in question are susceptible of two meanings: *Renfrewshire Assessor v Hendry* (1969) at 213. Alternatively, the words may be uncertain in scope and application: *Gordon v Kirkcaldy D.C.* (1990). The main aim of this process is to discover the intention of Parliament.

Statutory interpretation involves two general approaches. One adopts a literal, strict or narrow construction of terms and the other a more liberal or broader construction. Which of these two approaches is adopted depends on judicial choice and the earlier development of similar aspects of the law.

The former approach requires a close and careful scrutiny of the actual words of the statute. Words are to be used in their ordinary sense, as the words were used when the Act was passed. The latter approach emphasises the need for courts to try to appreciate the intention of the legislation and the need to provide a remedy rather than undertake a close textual analysis of some sort.

The literal approach gives rise to the "golden rule" of statutory interpretation, which is that the ordinary meaning of words should be seen to give the intention of Parliament, unless they result in a manifest absurdity: *IRC v Luke* (1963) at 80. A court may not disregard the plain meaning merely because it produces an anomaly, but only if it produces an absurdity: *Stock v Jones* (1978). That may, of course, apply to criminal statutes: *Strathern v Padden* (1926) at 13.

The liberal approach gives rise to the "mischief rule" which holds that as a statute was passed to remedy some mischief or defect in the law, an interpretation should be adopted which corrects the mischief: *e.g. Leadbetter v Hutcheson* (1934).

The Interpretation Act 1978 establishes in law meanings of words commonly found in statutes and many individual statutes give their own definitions which may be wider or narrower (or at least be different) from the ordinary discretionary meaning of the words.

It is important that interpretation has regard to the whole Act in which the phrase or word under construction appears, because the underlying

scheme or legislative purpose may support a particular meaning. Where a literal interpretation produces an absurd result the court must seek an interpretation more consistent with the Act: *Black v Glasgow Corporation* (1958).
Reference to the whole Act means regard is had to the whole context and in that respect there are now three principles:

(i) *noscitur a sociis*—a vague word takes a shade of meaning from the accompanying words;
(ii) *expression unius est exclusio alterius*—the express mention of one thing or category and not of another similar or related thing tends to indicate the implied exclusion of the latter;
(iii) *ejusdem generis*—where several things are listed and all have some common characteristic and the list is followed by words such as "or otherwise", it is to be presumed that the general words are limited to other items sharing the common characteristic.

Finally, the shades of meaning to be given to a word may also be discovered from internal and external aids to construction.

Internal aids are those indications which may be drawn from the relevant statute and these include the title, the preamble, the heading, the marginal notes, the interpretation statutes and the Schedules.

External aids are those sources of information outside the relevant statute. The principal external aids are the prior state of the law, earlier and later statutes, the case law, textbooks, dictionaries, and now, to a lesser extent, *Hansard* for statements made by Government Ministers: *Pepper v Hart* (1993); *Short's Trustees v Keeper of the Registers of Scotland* (1994).

A considerable body of presumptions has developed and these may be applied in the absence of anything to the contrary. A full consideration of all these presumptions is unnecessary here but reference to two of the more important, or at least better known, presumptions may be made.

First, statutes are presumed to have prospective effect only and not be retrospective so that Parliament can be said to have had only future cases in contemplation: *Scott v Aberdeen Corporation* (1976). However, a statute may be passed with the express intent of changing a decision of a court: the best, but not the only, example is the War Damage Act 1965 overruling *Burmah Oil Co Ltd v Lord Advocate* (1964).

Secondly, a strict construction is to be given to statutes restrictive of personal liberty or encroaching on the property rights of individuals: *Scott v Aberdeen Corporation* (1976).

PRECEDENT

Precedent and the common law are closely linked and precedent is a formal source of law. The authority of a rule of law thus created is the precedents from which it can be inferred, and not Parliament or any other legislature. In practice, the supreme courts can legislate. The operation of precedent is to be distinguished from the construction and interpretation of legislation where the courts apply the law laid down by a legislature. For a very full statement of judicial precedents see the opinion of Lord McCluskey in *Lord Advocate's reference No.1 of 2001* (2002). Precedents are cases which lay down rules or principles or extend existing principles. Precedents are created by judges in the course of deciding cases, to justify their decisions, and the rule is to be extracted from the written judgments. The rule as a statement of principle may have a profound sociological or moral sense. The system of precedents gives rise to three important concepts that are now considered.

Ratio decidendi

The *ratio decidendi* is the reason for a decision. The decision must be discoverable from the written judgment of the court. The *ratio decidendi*, or ratio, being law binds later judges under certain circumstances. Such binding means that the later judges must apply the rule or principle whether they wish to or not. There are four qualifications to be made to that proposition:

(1) No ratio stands alone. A decision by a court must be seen in the context of the common law and the surrounding law is not a matter that the judge can change.

(2) Ratios may differ because lawyers or commentators considering a written judgment may differ as to what principle is being established.

(3) Ratios fall to be considered later by other judges, and in determining later cases earlier ratios become the subject of decisions themselves and thus have their own importance or applicability varied.

(4) A ratio may be seen by later judges to be wrong, but whether it may be negated or applied depends very much on the court in which that ratio was established and whether the later court has any discretion in applying the ratio.

Identifying a *ratio decidendi* can be difficult, and that is particularly so where the judges reach the same result for different reasons: see, *e.g. Tudhope v McKee* (1987). Ascertaining the *ratio decidendi* of a case is a two-stage process. The first stage is to discover precisely what the decision was; the second stage is to discover what was the reasoning that was necessary to yield that decision: see Lord Advocate's Reference No.1 of 2001 (2002), *per* Lord McCluskey.

Obiter dicta

Obiter dicta usually means things said by the way or in passing. In analysing a written judgment for the *ratio decidendi* any discussion, observation or reasoning which does not form part of the ratio is obiter. As *obiter dicta* are not binding on the court, considerable effort in later cases may be put into seeking to argue that parts of the written judgment are *obiter dicta* rather than part of the *ratio decidendi*. Even if the ratio is clear, the *obiter dictum* may be highly persuasive in arguments in later cases.

Stare decisis

Stare decisis is the principle that courts must stand by what has been decided already. This essentially conservative doctrine seeks to promote certainty in the law as well as to avoid identical matters being litigated repeatedly. Certainty and consistency are different and *stare decisis* also promotes the latter.

Stare decisis in operation

Not all precedents are binding because not all precedents are relevant to later problems required to be solved by the courts. The *ratio decidendi* of a precedent requires to be in point with a matter then before a court. The prior decision is in point when there was raised, argued and decided in it to a certain set of facts some issue of law which is the same issue of law as arises in the new case before the court. Further, there is a hierarchy of courts and it is clear that a precedent in a lower court cannot bind a higher court. The hierarchy of the courts varies from legal system to legal system. For the present, one need be concerned only with the hierarchy of courts of relevant, or having some, jurisdiction in Scotland. These have been discussed earlier and a very brief outline of the principle of *stare decisis* in operation follows.

(1) The European Court is the supreme tribunal on matters of the interpretation of the Treaties of the European Union, the validity and interpretations of the legislation of the European Union and the interpretation of the statutes of bodies established by an Act of the Council. Decisions of the European Court are binding on all UK courts. The European Court does not regard itself as bound by its own previous decisions though it is slow to depart from its previous principles: *Da Costa* (1965).

(2) The House of Lords, when sitting as the final court of civil appeal from Scotland, sits as a Scottish court: *Cooper v Cooper* (1888); *Elliot v Joicey* (1935). The House of Lords normally considers itself bound by precedents of its own in Scottish appeals: *Oliver v Saddler* (1929) at 97. The House of Lords does not consider itself bound by dicta on questions of Scots law raised incidentally in English or Irish appeals: *Orr Ewing's Trs v Orr Ewing* (1885). It has been stated that the House of Lords may depart from previous decisions where it appears right to do so: practice note [1996] 3 All E.R. 77.

(3) Decisions of the Judicial Commitee of the Privy Council on devolution issues are binding on the courts: Scotland Act 1998, s.103(1).

(4) Either Division of the Inner House or an Extra Division of the Court of Session is normally bound by decisions of the House of Lords in

Scottish appeals: *Commerzbank AG v Large* (1977). These Divisions are also bound by a decision of seven or more judges of the Court of Session, and by a previous decision of any of the Divisions: *e.g. Marshall v Scottish Milk Marketing Board* (1956) at 39. A court of seven judges may overrule a precedent of either Division: *e.g. Scottish Discount Co v Blin* (1986). Changed social and economic conditions may make some precedents outmoded: see *Donnelly v Donnelly* (1959) at 102 and 103. Decisions of the House of Lords in English or Irish appeals are not binding but may be strongly persuasive: *Dalgleish v Glasgow Corporation* (1976) at 52.

(5) The High Court of Justiciary when dealing with appeals is not bound by decisions of the House of Lords in a criminal matter, even when dealing with a United Kingdom criminal statute: *Ritchie v Pirie* (1972) at 14; *Brennan v H.M. Advocate* (1977). Ordinarily any precedent doubted is reviewed by a larger, or even a full, bench: *e.g. Kirkwood v H.M. Advocate* (1939) (11 judges). Any full bench can overrule a quorum of three: *Anderson v H.M. Advocate* (1996).

(6) Court of Session, Outer House. A Lord Ordinary sitting alone in the Outer House is bound by decisions of the House of Lords in Scottish appeals and by decisions of seven or more judges: *Munro's Trs v Munro* (1971) at 284. Lords Ordinary are also bound by either Division or an Extra Division of the Inner House: *e.g. Hunter v Glasgow Corporation* (1971) at 231. Lords Ordinary are not bound by each other's decisions.

(7) Where the High Court of Justiciary sits as a trial court a Lord of Justiciary sitting alone is bound by the law as laid down previously on appeal by a bench of the High Court of Justiciary. It should be noted, however, that in any trial of difficulty or importance it is competent for two or more judges in the High Court of Justiciary to preside for the whole or any part of the trial: Criminal Procedure (Scotland) Act 1995, s.1(5). In *Copeland v H.M. Advocate* (1987) two other judges sat with a trial judge to deal with a point of law.

(8) Sheriffs principal and sheriffs are bound by decisions of the House of Lords: *Boosma v Clark and Rose Ltd* (1983). They are bound by the Inner House of the Court of Session. They are not bound by the decisions of the Outer House: *Farrell v Farrell* (1990). A decision by one sheriff does not bind another sheriff, although sheriffs will be bound by the sheriffs principal of that sheriffdom: *Lothian R.C. v T* (1984). One sheriff principal will not bind another sheriff principal: *Spencer v Spencer* (1983).

(9) A sheriff presiding at a trial by jury or trying a case summarily must apply the law as laid down by the High Court of Justiciary sitting in its appellate capacity: *Herron v Nelson* (1976). However, a sheriff is not necessarily bound by previous rulings of a single trial judge, either Lord of Justiciary or sheriff, though a sheriff will normally follow such rulings: *Jessop v Stevenson* (1988).

6. CIVIL LITIGATION

INTRODUCTION

It is wrong to think of all disputes as resulting in civil litigation. If the law is certain and, for example, the injury or harm done is admitted then the matter may be resolved without litigation. The threat of civil litigation, which might involve expense and publicity, often helps to resolve that which may be in dispute.

A civil dispute may arise where two or more parties are at issue on a matter of fact or law, or both, which affects their relevant legal rights and duties. The compromise, agreement or arbitration involved in the resolution of disputes is very much a matter of legal practice and is probably a universal part of lawyers□work throughout the world. What follows here, however, is a consideration of some of the civil proceedings that may be undertaken in Scotland to obtain a civil remedy.

A client may wish a particular result but the lawyer must have regard to various approaches in order to obtain the result. Civil remedies may be classified according to their purposes. The following list is not comprehensive but includes the principal remedies:

(1) *Declaratory judgments.* By these decisions the court declares that particular rights do or do not exist. It does not follow that the court makes a further order as to consequential action.

(2) *Reduction.* A court will reduce or set aside a contract, will, decree or other writing which then becomes invalid.

(3) *Prevention.* By this remedy a court orders the cessation of a legal wrong, either actual or intended, before any harm or further harm is done to the pursuer. An interdict is a common remedy in this regard and equates broadly with the English injunction.

(4) *Performance.* The court may order something to be done which ought otherwise to have been done under a legal duty. An example is an action of specific implement.

(5) *Damages.* The court may order financial compensation for loss, injury or harm caused by the failure to undertake a legal duty owed to the pursuer by the defender. Damages may be awarded in compensation for personal injuries sustained by the pursuer resulting from the defender□s fault.

(6) *Matrimonial remedies.* Actions of judicial separation may relieve a spouse from legal duties that ought to follow from marriage. Actions of divorce will end a marriage. These are sometimes known as consistorial remedies.

In the wide variety of circumstances giving rise to wrongs for which someone seeks a remedy, the distinction between questions of fact and questions of law must be observed. There are seldom circumstances which are exclusively matters of pure law. Equally, there are unlikely to be circumstances that are exclusively matters of fact. Most circumstances combine matters of fact and law.

It is said that in every set of circumstances there are four elements. First, there are rules of law and these are abstract and general. Secondly, there are facts and these are concrete and specific. Thirdly, there are human beings, who are complex and variable. Fourthly, there is the environment. This is to be seen in its broadest context and amounts to the background to the circumstances giving rise to a wrong. It is the accumulation of physical, social, cultural, intellectual, economic, political and industrial circumstances.

A question of fact concerns the existence in the past or present of some act or event or state of circumstances and these must be recognised or ascertained by human senses. A question of law concerns the existence or content or applicability of some doctrine, principle or rule of the legal system.

The importance of the distinction is pre-eminent: disputed questions of fact must be alleged in the written pleadings and the dispute must be decided upon by the judge (or the jury if there is one) after hearing the evidence. Disputed questions of law must be raised by appropriate pleas-in-law and are decided by the judge after hearing legal argument. Disputed questions of mixed fact and law are determined by the judge after hearing evidence of fact, and legal argument as to the consequences of the evidence being interpreted in one way or another. It is not unknown for circumstances to allow a jury verdict that amounts to a decision of a mixed question of fact and law.

The value of extensive written pleadings in civil litigation is that the points of dispute become clear before the actual trial or proof, thus narrowing the issues. The resolution of the disputed issues takes a different approach according to whether they are facts or law.

A disputed question of fact has to be determined by proof by adducing evidence of the events, namely what happened, was said, seen, heard or done. A disputed question of law, by contrast, is determined not by evidence but by legal argument, giving in support previous relevant decisions, statutes and related material.

It should also be mentioned in relation to disputed questions of fact that reliance is often placed on other branches of knowledge. There is probably no science or body of knowledge outside law which is not at some time relied on to explain or settle questions of facts in issue in a legal context. Of course, these practitioners from other disciplines do not themselves determine facts, but they do provide explanations, information and evidence on questions of fact to which principles of law can be applied. Some of these practitioners become experienced enough in court work to develop specialist titles, *e.g.* forensic odontologist.

Facts can also be distinguished themselves into acts and events. An act is a happening brought about by human activity, positive (by acting) or negative (by abstaining or refraining from acting). An event is a happening which occurs independently of human intervention. Moreover, a distinction is often drawn between fact and opinion. This is particularly so when an expert gives evidence. What a person has seen, heard or otherwise observed are facts. Guided by his or her professional knowledge he or she has then formed an opinion on the basis of these facts and that in itself is a fact, but the substance or content of the opinion itself is not a fact but a view reached by him or her.

These remedies that a court may provide, and the distinction between fact and law and the various consequences, apply to all civil actions in each of the courts. The emphasis varies, however, in each case because, to repeat a well-known legal principle, every case turns on its own facts and circumstances.

COURT OF SESSION

The Court of Session is the supreme civil court in Scotland. Proceedings are usually initiated in the Outer House by summons, although some actions commence by petition. A summons is a writ running in the name of the Queen and passed by the Signet; that is to say, it has been stamped to authenticate it.

A civil action is commenced by a pursuer and directed against a defender. The summons requires the defender, if there is any good reason why decree should not be pronounced, to appear in court to answer the allegations by the pursuer. The threat is that, without an appearance, the action may proceed without the defender and the pursuer will achieve the remedy sought.

The front page of the summons is a pre-printed form in which the parties are identified. This part is known as the instance. There then follows the brief statement of the precise remedy claimed. This part is known as the conclusion.

The remainder of the summons is divided into two parts. The condescendence consists of numbered paragraphs of facts which form the basis of the case. The number of paragraphs varies with the complexity of the circumstances. The pleas-in-law are the propositions of law upon which the pursuer bases his or her case.

The summons is signed by a solicitor entitled to practice before the Court of Session and signeted, or authenticated, at the court office. The defender is cited by having a copy of the summons served on him or her personally, or by post. The defender is allowed a certain period of time to answer the summons. This is known as the *induciae*. After that period has passed the summons is called by being listed in the Rolls of Court. The bundle of court papers, known as the process, is lodged for use in court.

A defender has two options. He or she may do nothing in which event the pursuer may take decree in absence against him. Alternatively, if the defender wishes to defend the case wholly or in part, he or she must enter appearance and then lodge defences. The defences are statements of fact which answer each part of the pursuer's document. In drafting defences the summons must be considered line by line and indicate whether each fact is admitted, denied or simply not known about. The defender must also set out his or her pleas-in-law for the court to be able to identify, taking the summons and defences together, the precise issue in each case. It follows that a defender may defend on the facts, or on the law, or both together.

The summons and defences together make up the open record and this document reproduces the summons, conclusions, the detailed condescendence with the precise answers by both sides and the pleas-in-law for each side. This document is then available for adjustment and that frequently requires to be done once each side becomes aware of the precise points made by the other. The ultimate aim is to adjust the written pleadings in order to give the other side fair warning of the grounds of the claim or defences, to identify the legal issues and to limit the evidence at any later hearing.

At the end of the period allowed for adjustments, the Lord Ordinary will pronounce an interlocutor closing the record. The final written pleadings then become the closed record, which incorporates the various adjustments made to the open record.

It is competent (that is to say, it is within the power of the court) to grant summary decree at this stage. This would be decree in favour of the pursuer and allowing the remedy sought. The court can only do that, however, where it is satisfied from the written pleadings in the closed record that there is no defence to the claim or a part of it.

Debate

The procedure of debate, or discussion on the legal aspects, may be contrasted with proof, which is the hearing of evidence from witnesses. The parties may be at issue on both law and fact. If the parties are at issue on a question of fact alone, the court will order a proof where a judge alone sits to decide upon the evidence, or a jury trial so that the jury can decide the issues: Court of Session Act 1988 (the 1988 Act), ss.9 and 11. There are 12 persons in a civil jury: 1988 Act, s.13. The case can also be sent to the procedure roll for a debate on whether a jury trial is appropriate.

If the parties wish to address a legal point arising from the pleadings the court will send the case to the procedure roll for a debate on the legal points raised by the pleas-in-law for the parties. When the case proceeds on that roll the debate proceeds on the law alone. The defender must at this stage accept for these purposes the pursuer's narration of the facts in the condescendence. For an example of such a case, see Appendix 2.

After the debate the judge may there and then give a decision but with the complexity of the issues frequently raised it is usual to make avizandum. This means giving a decision later and in writing. The nature and extent of that decision depends to a great extent on the issues that have been debated.

If the point of law is decided in favour of the defender the case may be ended at this point, or restricted. If the point of law is decided in favour of the pursuer the case may then proceed to proof or to jury trial. A further option is proof before answer, which means in effect that the circumstances of the case are such that any legal issues are reserved until the evidence is heard.

Proof

There are no opening speeches for either side. The pursuer, or the lawyer for the pursuer, calls the witnesses in support of the case. The benefit of the extensive written pleadings is that there is no need to prove any matter of fact admitted in the closed record. Careful drafting is necessary, because failure in the pleadings to deny an averment of fact within a party's knowledge is to be construed as an admission of fact.

At proof each witness takes or affirms an oath and is then examined-in-chief by the party who called the witness. The witness is then cross-examined by the lawyer for the other party, and then re-examined. The first stage determines the evidence of the witness, the second tests or challenges that evidence and allows the other party to explore such relevant matters as he chooses, and the third stage allows an opportunity to clear up any remaining matters of doubt. The judge may also intervene to clarify points of doubt. This procedure is undertaken for each witness called by each party.

The length of time that the proof takes depends on the facts and circumstances in issue, the need to prove them, the extent to which the parties agree evidence, the depth to which facts are explored and the intervention of the judge.

At the conclusion of all the evidence the lawyers for the parties address the court and make their submissions on the evidence and on the inferences to be drawn from it. While the judge could give a decision, it is usual to make avizandum. Later the opinion of the judge is issued and motions heard on awards of expenses if this cannot be agreed on. Decree granting or refusing the remedy sought is contained in the interlocutor.

Summary trial

The parties to any dispute or question may present a petition in the Outer House setting out the dispute or question, and asking that it may be decided by a particular Lord Ordinary: 1988 Act, s.26. The case may be determined in chambers. The decree is final and not appealable: *British Steamship Co v Lithgows Ltd* (1975). Summary trial is a convenient but rare means of obtaining a judicial construction of a deed or a writ: *Shaw v Shaw* (1968).

Jury trial

Jury trial is competent only in specified types of action, for example, an action of damages for personal injuries: 1988 Act, s.11. Even with these specified types of action the court may be persuaded that special reasons exist for hearing the case by proof rather than by jury trial: 1988 Act and see, *e.g. Meechan v McFarlane* (1996).

An issue is a question of fact formulated precisely in writing by the pursuer for the jury to answer. There may also be a counter-issue for the defender. These are designed to obtain an answer from the jury to the major matters of fact on which the parties are in dispute. There are opening speeches. The evidence is led in the same way as at a proof. At the conclusion of the evidence, the lawyers for the parties address the jury advocating their respective cases. The judge charges the jury on the law.

The verdict of the jury may be given unanimously or by a majority. The verdict is normally a general verdict by giving answers to the questions in the issue or in the counter-issue. A special verdict may follow if a specific question is put to a jury. The verdict is recorded and the jury discharged and the lawyer for the party for whom the jury have decided then moves the court to apply the verdict and this allows decree to be granted.

Reclaiming motions

Any party to a cause initiated in the Outer House either by a summons or a petition who is dissatisfied with an interlocutor may reclaim (appeal to the Inner House) against that interlocutor: 1988 Act, s.28. These appeals may challenge the Lord Ordinary's opinion on the law and one may also reclaim a decision on the facts: *e.g. Islip Pedigree Breeding Centre v Abercromby* (1959).

Any party who is dissatisfied with the verdict of the jury in any jury action may apply to the Inner House for a new trial on various statutory grounds, e.g. misdirection of the jury by the judge: 1988 Act, s.29.

Appeals from the sheriff court are also heard by the Inner House and disposed of in the same way as reclaiming motions. These appeals (like reclaiming motions and applications for new trials) appear on the rolls of either Division of the Inner House and the judges have before them prints of the sheriff court record and interlocutors.

Petitions

Petitions may be presented to the Outer House. Petitions for judicial review of administrative actions are now competent. Some kinds of petitions, however, are presented directly to the Inner House. The petitions to the *nobile officium* of the Court of Session proceed to the Inner House as they constitute a request for the exercise of an extraordinary equitable remedy where the law is otherwise silent as to the correction of a wrong.

HOUSE OF LORDS

An appeal against a decision of the Inner House may be taken to the House of Lords: 1988 Act, s.40. Appeals may be taken on grounds of fact or law. Appeals on fact are difficult because the Law Lords are not readily prepared to differ on an issue of fact from the view of the judge who saw and heard the witnesses: *Martinez v Grampian Health Board* (1996).

An appeal takes the form of a petition and a joint statement of facts and issues, and an appendix must also be included with all the relevant court papers and the opinions of the judges in the other courts. The judgment of the House of Lords is returned to the Inner House, where that judgment is applied.

SHERIFF COURT

Ordinary causes

The principles of pleading and procedure in the Court of Session have been sent out at some length above. They apply in a generally similar way in the sheriff court but with some variation. Most proceedings are governed by the Ordinary Cause Rules issued by the Court of Session by Act of Sederunt. An action is commenced by an initial writ, petition or summons and the relevant document requires a warrant from the sheriff clerk. Civil jury trial in the sheriff court was abolished in 1980.

Summary causes

A summary cause action can only be raised in the sheriff court. If it relates to the payment of money it is used where the value of the claim is over £750 and up to (and including) £1,500. The most common type is for payment of money, but another example is an action to recover occupation of property. These actions are commenced with the completion of a standard printed form with an annexed statement of claim containing a statement of facts. There is a right of appeal to the sheriff principal on points of law, but not on facts.

Small claims

A small claim action can only be raised in the Sheriff Court. It is used where the value of the claim is up to (and including) £750. There are three types of claim that can be raised under this procedure: (i) a claim for payment of money; (ii) a claim for delivery of moveable property; and (iii) a claim for implementation of an obligation. These actions must be commenced with the completion of a standard form with an annexed statement of claim containing a statement of facts. There is a right of appeal to the sheriff principal on points of law, but not on facts.

Sheriff court appeals

Appeal is competent from the judgment of the sheriff or sheriff principal by means of a note of appeal signed by the appellant. Thereafter, appeal may be competent to the Court of Session by note of appeal against final judgments of either sheriff or sheriff principal: see Sheriff Courts (Scotland) Act 1971, s.38.

DILIGENCE

The process of putting an order of the court into effect is known as diligence. In Scots law the term [judgment☐has no technical or precise meaning, and is used to refer to almost every aspect of a decision or determination of a case, including the opinions of the judges or the court. The technical terms normally applied to the operative aspects of judgments are interlocuters and decrees. The distinction between these terms is that an interlocuter is an incidental order of a court issued in the course of a cause, whereas a decree is the court order that finally disposes of a cause.

LAW OF EVIDENCE

In civil proceedings the court or jury, if satisfied that any fact has been established by evidence in those proceedings, is entitled to find that fact proved notwithstanding that the evidence is not corroborated: Civil Evidence (Scotland) Act 1988 s.1. Evidence is concerned with proof, not of cases, but of facts. Crucial facts are the *facta probanda*, the facts that (in a civil case) a party must aver in order to make a case relevant to be sent to proof. The crucial facts in any civil cause ought to be discoverable from the written pleadings. In civil cases the standard to be met is a balance of probabilities.

---

7. CRIMINAL JUSTICE

INTRODUCTION

The administration of criminal justice in any legal system is dependent on several areas of the law; the criminal law itself is, of course, central to the task and that law varies from one jurisdiction to another. The manner in which the administration is carried out is heavily dependent on the criminal procedure, the rules to be applied in and prior to court appearances, and the criminal law of evidence, the rules of how facts are to be proved or admitted. The attainment of justice is thus achieved by an intimate mixture of criminal law, evidence and procedure. The activities of lawyers in practice are determined by this law, evidence and procedure, and that is equally so for civil and criminal work. It must also be said that lawyers in practice deal with clients legal problems without necessarily considering each of these areas individually and separately: the academic divisions of the law need not necessarily parallel law in practice.

PUBLIC PROSECUTION

Private prosecution is competent in Scots law and may result in trial by jury: *e.g. X v Sweeney* (1982). It may also bring about trial without jury: *e.g. Caven v Cumming* (1998). However, a principal feature of criminal proceedings is that public prosecution is the general rule and private prosecution is rare.

The Lord Advocate is the supreme public prosecutor: see *Dumfries C.C. v Phyn* (1895). The Lord Advocate is assisted by the Solicitor-General for Scotland and by a number of Advocates Depute, known collectively as Crown Counsel. The Lord Advocate and the Solicitor General are appointed by the Government of the day. Crown Counsel work from Crown Office in Edinburgh and there are a number of permanent officials there who, as civil servants, provide the continuity at the centre of the system.

The senior permanent official is the Crown Agent who is in the position of managing director of the department: the Deputy Crown Agent deals mainly with operational matters. The department is in essence the Procurator Fiscal Service. The permanent local public prosecutor is the procurator fiscal, and each is appointed by the Lord Advocate and subject to direction as appropriate by Crown Counsel.

All prosecutions commenced in Scotland by the public prosecutors are done so in the public interest and there must be sufficient evidence for that to happen: a sufficiency of evidence, or corroboration, is central to the decision to prosecute. Public prosecutors also decide the forum, or court, in which a case is to proceed.

SOLEMN AND SUMMARY PROCEDURE

The decision as to forum is essentially between solemn and summary procedure. Solemn procedure is trial on indictment before a judge at the High Court of Justiciary and a jury of 15 people, or before a sheriff principal or sheriff also with a jury of 15 people. Summary procedure is trial on complaint before a sheriff principal or a sheriff, or a stipendiary magistrate, or one or more justices of the peace, but without a jury.

The factors to which public prosecutors must have regard in deciding upon forum vary from case to case. First, the High Court of Justiciary has exclusive jurisdiction in cases of treason, murder, rape, incest, deforcement of messengers, breach of duty by magistrates, and certain cases of statutory offences.

Secondly, as judges, sheriffs and magistrates have sentencing powers of varying degrees, the more serious a crime appears to be the more appropriate it becomes that a particular allegation should be tried in a higher court. It is a general rule but not an invariable principle that the more serious crimes attract the heaviest sentences.

Thirdly, many individuals who are to be tried have previous convictions that require to be taken into consideration on being sentenced for later criminal behaviour. Modest or even trivial crimes may be tried on indictment to allow greater powers of sentencing to the trial judge. A man may, for example, have been sentenced to a long period of imprisonment for supplying controlled drugs. To return to such unlawful activity on release may result in a prosecution in a higher forum than the later crime necessarily merits in itself.

Fourthly, the terms of a statute may require that a particular forum is envisaged: thus vandalism is an offence which can only be prosecuted summarily because no provision is made for sentence on indictment: Criminal Law (Consolidation) (Scotland) Act 1995, s.52(3). The point is narrow for many statutory offences can easily be prosecuted as common law crimes to avoid such restrictions: vandalism may be charged as malicious damage.

These decisions, and others, are taken by the Crown, the general name for the prosecution. As public prosecutors in Scotland are not police prosecutors, the decisions are taken independently of the police. The police complete their investigations by submitting a report to the procurator fiscal for consideration. The interests of the public and the Crown are, or should be, consistent with each other but they are not identical. The police in Scotland do not prosecute in court.

The independent nature of the public prosecutor is emphasised further by the regular receipt by the procurator fiscal of reports for consideration for prosecution from many other agencies. Some 40 or so non-police agencies, such as the Department of Social Security or local authorities, submit reports and these are dealt with on the same principle as police cases.

One important difference ought to be noted. The police are required to make such reports to the procurator fiscal: Police (Scotland) Act 1967, s.17(1). The procurator fiscal has the power to direct the police: 1967 Act, proviso to s.17(3). The non-police reporting agencies, however, need not report matters to the procurator fiscal who in turn has no power to direct them.

Solemn procedure

Any crime or offence which is triable on indictment may be tried by the High Court of Justiciary sitting at any place in Scotland: the Criminal Procedure (Scotland) Act 1995 (hereafter the □1995 Act□), s.3(2). A judge in the High Court of Justiciary is a judge of the Supreme Court, and he or she may thus impose any sentence provided that the sentence is not in excess of the maximum competent sentence. A sheriff is not entitled on the conviction on indictment of an accused to pass a sentence of imprisonment for a term exceeding three years: 1995 Act, s.3(3).

Petition

Solemn procedure is commenced with the procurator fiscal presenting a petition to a sheriff. That petition identifies the accused, the charge under consideration and seeks a warrant to arrest the accused, to search him or her and the premises where the accused is found, and authority to cite witnesses for precognition.

The authority sought by such a warrant does not exclude any other common law or statutory power of arrest. The petition warrant is also separate from the warrant that may be sought for special inquiry, *e.g.* a warrant to take dental impressions: *Hay v H.M. Advocate* (1968). A warrant may be sought for a blood sample: *H.M. Advocate v Milford* (1973).

A petition for a warrant to arrest and commit a person suspected of or charged with a crime proceeds as set out in s.34 of the 1995 Act.

First appearance or first examination

On being arrested an accused person is entitled to have intimation of his or her detention, and the details of the place where he or she is being detained, sent to a solicitor and to one other person reasonably named by him or her without delay, or with minimum delay in the public interest: 1995 Act, s.15(1)(b) and s.17. There are now statutory powers to take prints, samples, etc.: 1995 Act, s.18.

As soon as possible after arrest, the accused is brought before a sheriff for examination and that should take place on the next lawful court day after arrest that is not a Saturday, Sunday or court holiday.

The first appearance on a petition warrant is normally brief and formal and in private. The accused may state a plea or make a declaration (a statement), but in practice that is now rare.

A procurator fiscal may have an accused brought to court for judicial examination; that is the accused may be questioned by the prosecutor in so far as such questions are directed to eliciting any admission, denial, explanation, justification or comment: 1995 Act, s.36. The accused□s solicitor shall be entitled to be present: 1995 Act, s.35. The record of the judicial examination may be put in evidence at a subsequent trial: *e.g. Moran v H.M. Advocate* (1990).

After the first appearance or first examination the accused may either be committed for further examination or committed until liberated in due course of law (also committed for trial). The distinction is important because if just the former happens then the prosecutor must ensure that the accused is in due course committed for trial unless he or she is released on bail. The length of time between first appearance or first examination and committal for trial is usually about a week. If an accused has been committed for further examination and then liberated on bail it is not necessary to commit him or her until liberated in due course of law: 1995 Act, s.23(3).

These procedures are important for the timings of prosecutions. First, committal for further examination and bail requires a trial to be commenced within 12 months of the first appearance of the accused on petition: 1995 Act, s.65(1). Secondly, committal until liberation in due course of law with the accused remanded in custody requires a trial to be commenced within 110 days of the date of that full committal: 1995 Act, s.65(4)(b).

Any person accused on petition of a crime which is by law bailable is entitled immediately on the occasion on which he or she is brought before the sheriff prior to committal until liberation in due course of law, to apply to the sheriff for bail: 1995 Act, s.23(1). All crimes and offences except murder and treason are bailable: 1995 Act, s.24(1).

The indictment

If after investigation there is to be a trial by jury an indictment is prepared and signed. The indictment is in the name of the Lord Advocate in the High Court or on the authority of the Lord Advocate in the sheriff court. The form of the indictment is set out in law: see the 1995 Act, s.65 and Sch.2.

After the indictment is served on the accused there may be a preliminary diet in the High Court case: 1995 Act, s.72. There must be a first diet in the sheriff court case: 1995 Act, s.71. The essence of these diets is to consider preliminary points or to try to agree evidence.

The trial

At the trial diet the accused is required to plead guilty or not guilty and a jury of 15 is balloted from the potential jurors present (the assize). Before a juror is sworn in, the prosecutor and the defence may excuse that juror from service without giving a reason: 1995 Act, s.86(1). An objection may be stated with a reason: 1995 Act, s.86(2).

There are no opening speeches. The evidence is taken from the prosecution witnesses by the prosecutor and the defence may test that evidence and explore other evidence in cross-examination. At the end of the Crown case it may be said by the defence that there is insufficient evidence to justify a conviction; that is to say, that there is no case to answer: 1995 Act, s.97(1). If the case proceeds, the accused may give evidence but need not necessarily do so. In speeches to the jury the defence speaks last: 1995 Act, s.98.

A special defence is a fact which, if established, must lead to the acquittal of the accused of the charge on the indictment: *Adam v McNeill* (1971). That defence is required to be stated timeously: 1995 Act, s.78. The jury must be informed of the special defence: 1995 Act, s.89. The special defences are alibi, insanity, incrimination and self-defence.

The verdict of the jury, given after the judge or sheriff has advised them of the law to be applied, is given orally by the foreman or forewoman: 1995 Act, s.100(1). The three possible verdicts are guilty, not guilty and not proven. The accused may only be convicted if at least eight of the 15 jurors have voted for guilty: *McPhelin v H.M. Advocate* (1960).

Appeals from solemn proceedings

A person convicted on indictment after trial by jury in the High Court of Justiciary or the sheriff court may appeal to the High Court of Justiciary sitting for the disposal of appeals and other proceedings: 1995 Act, s.103. An appeal may be against conviction or sentence or in regard to other orders of the court: 1995 Act, s.106.

By an appeal (using a note of appeal) a person may bring under review of the High Court of Justiciary any alleged miscarriage of justice, which may include a miscarriage based on the existence and significance of evidence which was not heard at the original proceedings and the jury's having returned a verdict which no reasonable jury, properly directed by the judge or sheriff, could have returned: 1995 Act, s.106(3).

The High Court of Justiciary may dispose of an appeal against conviction by affirming the verdict of the trial court, setting aside the verdict of the trial court and either quashing the conviction or substituting for it an amended verdict, or setting aside the verdict and granting authority for a new prosecution: 1995 Act, s.118(1). There are similar powers in regard to appeals against sentence: 1995 Act, s.118(3).

Summary procedure

All courts of criminal jurisdiction in Scotland, except the High Court of Justiciary, have a summary procedure. Under this procedure a sheriff, a stipendiary magistrate or others, sit without a jury to decide both matters of fact and points of law.

A sheriff sitting summarily has extensive powers of sentencing which, without prejudice to wider powers in other statutes, include a fine not exceeding £5,000, a requirement to find money (caution) or security for good behaviour for a period not exceeding 12 months, and to imprison for up to three months: 1995 Act, s.5(2). Where a person is convicted by the sheriff of a second or subsequent offence inferring dishonest appropriation of property, or an attempt to do so, or a second or subsequent offence inferring personal violence, the court may imprison for up to six months: the 1995 Act, s.5(3).

The sheriff court has jurisdiction to try all common law offences except murder, rape, incest and wilful fire-raising, and also statutory offences, except where jurisdiction is expressly or impliedly excluded: *Wilson v Hill* (1943).

A district court, without prejudice to any other or wider powers in other statutes, is entitled on convicting of a common law offence to impose imprisonment for a period not exceeding 60 days or to impose a fine not exceeding £2,500: 1995 Act, s.7(6). However, a district court when constituted by a stipendiary magistrate has the summary criminal jurisdiction and powers of a sheriff: 1995 Act, s.7(5).

These statutory powers impose a degree of constraint but otherwise the decision as to which court a case is to proceed in lies with the Lord Advocate and the procurator fiscal.

In Scotland the Crown prosecutes in the public interest and not for some narrow or vexatious purpose. The justice or the merits of some minor incident may suggest consideration of alternatives to prosecution. A warning letter may be sent, or a fixed penalty, in the form of a conditional offer, may be made. The latter allows for a payment within a period of time instead of prosecution: 1995 Act, s.302. This and other similar approaches remove from the courts cases at the lower end of seriousness.

Complaint

Summary proceedings require the service of a summary complaint on the accused. In the vast number of prosecutions the procurator fiscal is the complainer and the prosecution is carried out in the name of the procurator fiscal. Attached to a summary complaint there should be a schedule of any previous convictions which is intended to be put before the court in the event of a plea of guilty or a finding of guilt by the court: see the 1995 Act, Pt IX generally.

Intermediate diet

An intermediate diet is required to be held before the actual trial. The purpose of the intermediate diet is to ascertain whether a trial is likely to proceed on the trial date and also to ascertain the state of preparation of the prosecutor and the accused, whether the accused still pleads not guilty and the extent to which evidence can be agreed as being uncontentious: 1995 Act, s.148.

Trial

No part of a trial may take place outwith the presence of the accused: 1995 Act, s.154. Once the trial has begun the prosecution calls witnesses in support of the charge and the witnesses may be cross-examined by the accused or his or her lawyer. The summary complaint may be amended so as to cure any error or defect in it, to meet any objection to it or to cure any discrepancy or variance between the complaint and the evidence: 1995 Act, s.159. Immediately after the close of the evidence for the prosecution, the accused may submit that he or she has no case to answer: 1995 Act, s.160.

Appeals from summary proceedings

Either party to a summary prosecution may, on the final determination, apply to the court to state a case for the opinion of the High Court of Justiciary. Such an appeal may be against conviction or sentence or in regard to other orders of the court: 1995 Act, s.175.

By an appeal a person may bring under review of the High Court of Justiciary any alleged miscarriage of justice, which may include a miscarriage based on the existence and significance of evidence which was not heard at the original proceedings: 1995 Act, s.175(5).

The High Court of Justiciary may dispose of a stated case by (a) remitting the matter to the trial court with its opinion and any direction; (b) affirming the decision of the trial court; (c) setting aside the original verdict and either quashing the conviction or substituting their own verdict; or (d) setting aside the original verdict and granting authority to bring a new prosecution: 1995 Act, s.183(1).

Appeals may be taken against sentence only by means of a note of appeal: 1995 Act, s.186(1). That and the other statutory means of appeal do not exclude other common law means of appeal such as Bills of Suspension or Advocation: 1995 Act, s.191.

COMMON LAW APPEALS

Suspension is the procedure whereby an illegal or improper warrant, conviction or judgment from a lower court dealing with summary criminal procedures may be reviewed and set aside by the High Court of Justiciary. This procedure is not available to trials on indictment: *Outram v Lees* (1992). Generally this is a remedy open only to a person accused or convicted and not to a prosecutor.

Advocation may be used by the accused but it is normally used by the prosecutor: *Macleod v Levitt* (1969). In essence an accused may present a Bill if there has been a fundamental nullity or flagrant breach of fundamental principles of justice. The prosecution may proceed if there has been a serious mistake with the case at the court of first instance.

The *nobile officium* is the inherent equitable power of the High Court of Justiciary to deal with extraordinary or unforeseen circumstances, or where there is no other common law or statutory remedy: *Wan Ping Nam v German Minister of Justice* (1972); *Black v H.M. Advocate* (1991). A petition may also proceed where there is no other means of review which appears competent or appropriate: *Anderson v H.M. Advocate* (1974).

LAW OF EVIDENCE

The rules of evidence are more strictly applied in criminal cases than they are in civil cases. The Crown must prove the charge on indictment or on summary complaint beyond reasonable doubt. Moreover there is always a question of sufficiency of evidence, which means, in practice, that every essential fact must be corroborated. By corroboration it is meant that the evidence must be supported by independent evidence from other sources. Corroboration amounts to an independent check on the evidence. Not every fact must be corroborated, only those facts that go to proving the commission of a crime and the identification of the accused as a person responsible for committing the crime charged. In civil cases the standard is a balance of probabilities and corroboration is not essential.

---

8. THE FUTURE

This work has been about the Scottish legal system. The quotation of John Rawls set out at the beginning is as applicable to our system as it is to any other, in that certainty is necessary in order to define the boundaries of liberties. And yet a legal system is not and never has been static. What is true of our legal system is probably true of many other aspects of contemporary life: change has always been inevitable but the speed of change in our era is faster than it was in the past, and possibly more profound. What follows is a brief discussion of elements of the Scottish legal system where change has started, will continue and may be of great importance.

THE SCOTTISH PARLIAMENT

The United Kingdom has a highly complex historical inheritance. Despite that, however, the United Kingdom has had a unitary constitution since 1707, characterised by a single sovereign legislature and a central government. This type of government is characterised by a hierarchical relationship between central and local government. The distribution of powers in a federal government, for example, is frequently, perhaps even invariably, contained in a written constitution. The demarcation of powers between the parts of the federation is often regulated by a constitutional or a supreme court.

The Scotland Act 1998, speaking metaphorically, has the same effect on the constitution as introducing a new cantilever into the Forth Bridge: all existing relationships take on a different perspective and, in the short term at least, the smoothness and balance become disrupted.

The greater context of the Scotland Act 1998 is best left for consideration by and advice from constitutional lawyers, especially until political conventions have developed allowing for a clearer understanding of how Members of the Scottish Parliament ("MSPs") wish the Scottish constitution to work in practice.

It should be noted, however, that at least two developments may lead to a reconsideration of the personnel and functions within the Scottish legal system. First, the 1998 Act provides for a mechanism whereby an Act of the Scottish Parliament can be said by any court or tribunal to be outwith the legislative competence of the Scottish Parliament or a member of the Scottish executive: see s.91 and Sch.6 of the 1998 Act. Broadly, any court or tribunal may remit a restricted or devolution issue to the Inner House of the Court of Session for determination. Equally, any court consisting of three or more judges of the Court of Session may refer any devolution issue which arises in proceedings before it to the Judicial Committee of the Privy Council. The practical effect of these developments, it may reasonably be argued at this early stage, is to introduce into the Scottish legal system a role for the Judicial Committee that amounts in effect to a role of a constitutional court to determine the *vires* or powers of the Scottish Parliament. The Judicial Committee thus far has ordinarily sat in London.

Secondly, the role of the law officers will change materially. The 1998 Act in law returns to the position long before the Act of Union in that the Lord Advocate, *ex officio*, is a Member of the Scottish Parliament. Standing orders will determine the extent of such participation by the Lord Advocate and the Solicitor General for Scotland. The Law Officers are in any event members of the Scottish executive: s.41(1)(c) of the 1998 Act.

The principal Scottish legal adviser to the Government of the United Kingdom will be the Advocate General for Scotland. The Scottish legal system of the immediate future will thus have three Law Officers in place of the traditional two. The Advocate General has a power, equal to that of the Lord Advocate for Scotland and the Attorney General for England and Wales, to refer a question of *vires* to the Judicial Committee of the Privy Council.

The importance of these changes is, at the very least, that there will require to be a re-ordering of the nature and extent of rights, duties and responsibilities of the Law Officers. This change will take place in the context of an enhanced position of constitutional law.

RIGHTS OF AUDIENCE

From time immemorial advocates have had a monopoly on the right to appear in the Supreme Courts of Scotland to represent clients. That right of audience was extended to certain solicitors by virtue of s.24A of the Solicitors (Scotland) Act 1980. The right was also extended to any person who has complied with the terms of a scheme approved under s.26 of the Law Reform (Miscellaneous Provisions) (Scotland) Act 1990. In practice, few solicitors have taken the opportunity to obtain extended rights of audience and fewer still have actually exercised their rights.

As indicated earlier, a Reporter to the Children's Panel with at least one year's experience is entitled to conduct certain proceedings in a sheriff court. Such a Reporter may have a qualification as a social worker rather than as a lawyer. That may be seen by some as an encroachment on the rights of lawyers. Such developments do not necessarily occur in isolation and one might well look to see changes in other jurisdictions. Thus, for example, the Crime and Disorder Act 1998, s.53, allows designated members of staff of the Crown Prosecution Service to undertake certain court duties in England and Wales.

The tendency to change rights of audience between lawyers in a divided profession or to introduce non-lawyers into courts to conduct proceedings when this has not been done before is a major development. The nature and extent of this change across various jurisdictions, and in Scotland in particular, could have important repercussions for the future.

THE PUBLIC DEFENDER

Accused persons generally have legal representation except when appearing on minor matters. That legal representation might be at the expense of the accused or, more commonly, has been made available at public expense. In the latter instance, the solicitors used all to be from private practice. However, parliamentary authority was given by s.50 of the Crime and Punishment (Scotland) Act 1997 to implement the Public Defence Solicitors' Office. Public funds were made available on a five-year pilot scheme basis to test the viability of providing the public requiring state-funded legal assistance in criminal cases with an alternative to private practice solicitors. Subsequent statutory changes have given the Public Defence Solicitors' Office an indefinite life span with no restrictions now on either the number of solicitors that may be employed or the geographical location in which they operate.

ALTERNATIVE DISPUTE RESOLUTION

Virtually any dispute may be resolved in court by one procedure or another. Litigation, however, has its advantages and disadvantages, and these are often in practice considered and balanced against each other before proceeding to court.

The advantages of court procedure include; first, the existence of a known body of law on matters of dispute and also established procedural rules to ensure fairness and balance. The regularity of disputes means that there are precedents which assist with achieving a proper settlement.

Secondly, those precedents and the accumulated experience of judges and lawyers taken together means that disputes do not meet courts which are new to the subject matter.

Thirdly, disputes—commercial or personal—can become very bitter and the existing law and experience and the training of lawyers results, it may reasonably be said, in an objective approach. This, in practice, may mean the offering of detached advice that is not what a client wants to hear, but pandering to the subjective aspect is likely in the long run to result in even greater problems.

Fourthly, the orders or the decisions of the court may be enforced: an order to deliver something must be followed otherwise the court has powers or sanctions to impose upon the defaulting party. The implementation of a decision, therefore, does not depend necessarily on the acquiescence or goodwill of the other party.

The disadvantages of court procedures are well known. First, instructions to solicitors and counsel and the necessary preparation for litigation means expense. It is true that these costs may, if successful, be recovered. However, success is seldom guaranteed and it does not follow that the losing party will be able to pay the costs. Intending litigants may be required to put their lawyers in funds in order to commence proceedings.

Secondly, the thoroughness needed for court work combined with the pressure on the courts means that actions may be slow. The right of appeal, especially in the civil context with the House of Lords as the final court, lays open the possibility of long delay as the case proceeds.

Thirdly, the law of evidence affects the admissibility of, and the means of determining, facts. The need for, or the absence of a requirement for, corroboration is an example of rules that may affect the chances of success. There are sound reasons for having evidential rules: fairness for example. But the existence of such complex rules may not be conducive to resolving minor or comparatively minor disputes.

Fourthly, those rules taken with detailed procedural rules means that a case may fall on a matter other than the merits of the subject matter. Litigation may conceivably end without an actual resolution of the dispute or the point at issue.

Alternative dispute resolution ("ADR") is simply a series of alternatives for resolving differences without the need to go to court. These approaches may be informal arrangements covering community or business mediation, trade association, conciliation or arbitration schemes, employment disputes, ombudsmen and similar regulatory schemes. These may be offered, accordingly, on a United Kingdom or Scottish level or within particular groups of people.

This approach generally has been actively encouraged by many organisations including, ironically it may be thought, the publication in 1996 of a booklet entitled *Resolving Disputes Without Going to Court* by the Scottish Courts Administration. The removal of litigation from the courts is of more than passing interest to lawyers. Yet, while ADR has been promoted, doubts remain as to its viability in the long term. The Scottish Office Central Research Unit published research findings of a survey which examined the nature and extent of ADR in Scotland, and which identified the key issues relevant to the future development of ADR.

The findings included the point that the commonest form of ADR in operation was mediation and that there were then about 130 trained lawyer mediators operating in Scotland. There was, however, little evidence uncovered of actual ADR practice in any field except that of family law.

The views as to the reasons for the lack of ADR activity were varied. Some of those taking part in the survey thought that both lawyers and the wider public were simply not aware of what ADR involves or that it was available. Others who responded felt that there was evidence of resistance, both from lawyers and the public, to the acceptance of ADR: see 1996 S.L.T. (News) 342.

There is considerable literature on ADR schemes and strong supporters of individual schemes. It may be that enthusiasm for ADR has outrun its practical development. It is certain, however, that alternatives to the traditional forensic resolution of disputes are now established to some degree, although the full importance is yet to be established.

APPENDIX ONE

GLOSSARY AND LATIN MAXIMS AND PHRASES

There has been a definite move to try to use plain and simple English wherever possible in relation to legal matters. It remains true, however, that all trades and professions have some technical terms. The glossary here sets out some of the common words which have a particular relevance for lawyers.

Latin is used less now than it may have been in the past. The brief Latin phrase, it must be said, often encapsulates a somewhat complex legal concept. It is for this reason that a brief list of maxims is set out below.

GLOSSARY

Absolvitor: the judgment pronounced when a court assoilzies (*q.v.*).

Adhere: (1) of husband and wife, to remain with and be faithful to the other; (2) of a court, to affirm the judgment of a lower court.

Adjust: in a civil action, there is an initial "adjustment" period when the parties can make changes in their written pleadings. At this stage the "record" is "open". After the adjustment period the "record is closed". Any subsequent changes are by "amendment".

Advise: to give a considered judgment in a case: see *avizandum*.

Aggravation: some detail in a criminal change which, if proved, makes conviction more serious, *e.g.* assault to severe injury rather than merely assault to injury.

Agnate: a person related through the father.

Aliment: support or maintenance of a wife or relative enforceable by law.

Answer: a written pleading given in to a court usually in reply to a claim.

Appellant: a person appealing to higher court against decision of lower court.

Arbiter: a person chosen freely by parties to a dispute to decide a difference between them.

Assoilzie: to absolve, or decide finally in favour of, a defender.

Aver: to state or allege, especially in written pleadings.

Avizandum: taking time to consider a judgment.

Before answer: before the law of a case is decided. When a proof before answer is allowed, the facts are heard but the legal argument that the facts do not entitle relief is still competent.

Bond: a written obligation to pay money.

Books of Adjourned: the books or records of the Justiciary Court.

Books of Council and Session: a more common name for the Registers of Deeds and Probative Writs.

Books of Sederunt: the records of the Acts of Sederunt of the Court of Session.

Caution: security for a future action.

Cite: to summon to court, whether of party, witness or juror.

Cognate: a relative through the mother.

Conclusion: the statement of the precise relief sought.

Construction: interpretation. Verb is to construe, *i.e.* interpret.

Damnum: loss. *Damnum injuria data* means loss caused by the wrongdoing of another person.

Declarator, action of: an action brought by a party to have some legal right declared but without a claim on the defender to do anything.

Decree: the final judgment of a Scottish court.

Defender: the party against whom a civil action is brought.

Delict: a civil wrong.

Extract: a written statement of a decree

Fee: the full right of property in heritage: *q.v.* liferent.

Heritage: property in the form of land or houses.

Interdict: a judicial prohibition from a Scottish court.

Judicial factor: a person appointed by court to administer property, investments etc. for some special reason.

Jus commune: the common law of much of mediaeval and early modern Europe, based on Roman, canon and feudal law.

Liferent: the use of a property by a person during his or her own life.

Locus standi: see "title to sue".

Notary public: a public office also held by a solicitor.

Parole evidence: oral evidence.

Prescription: the passing of a period of time which either confers rights or cuts them off or alters them.

Pursuer: the person suing in a court action.

Real right: a right in a thing, as opposed to a right against a person.

Reclaim: to appeal to the Inner House of the Court of Session against the decision of an Outer House judge.

Reparation: the correcting of a civil wrong, usually by an award of damages.

Resile: (a) to withdraw from an agreement before it has become a binding contract; (b) to withdraw from a contract.

Solatium: damages to compensate for suffering, as opposed to patrimonial loss, which is loss of an economic position.

Specific implement: remedy of getting someone to perform an obligation itself, as opposed to damages for its non-performance.

Sustain: if a court sustains an argument, that means it accepts it. Opposite of "repel".

Title to sue: one possible defence to a claim is that the pursuer has no title to sue, *i.e.* even if the defender has acted unlawfully, the right to object is vested in someone other than the pursuer. Also called *locus standi*.

LATIN MAXIMS AND PHRASES

A coelo usque ad centrum: from the heavens to the centre of the earth.

A fortiori: by a stronger argument; so much the more.

A mensa et thoro: from bed and board. A decree of separation of this nature does not end a marriage, but merely releases one spouse from certain legal duties.

A vinculo matrimonii: from the bond of marriage. A divorce *a vinculo* ends a marriage as if it never existed.

Actus non facit reum, nisi mens sit rea: the act does not make the performer of it a criminal, unless there is also criminal evidence.

Ad factum praestandum: for the performance of a certain act. A decree of a court is of this class if it requires something to be done.

Ad vitam aut culpam: for life or until fault.

Audi alteram partem: one of the "rules of natural justice", namely that the other party has a right to be heard.

Bona vacantia: the goods of persons dying without successors. These goods become the property of the Crown as *ultimus haeres q.v.*

Brevitatis causa: for the sake of brevity. To refer to a document in this way is to import it into another document without copying it out.

Casus improvisus: an unforeseen case.

Contra bones mores: against morality.

Damnum injuria datum: damage or injury culpably inflicted.

Delectus personae: a choice of person to the exclusion of others.

Delegata potestas non potest delegari: a delegated power cannot be delegated.

Lex nil furstra facit: the law does nothing in vain. Orders of the court, for example, are intended to have effect.

Lex non cogit ad impossibilia: the law does not require the performance of what is impossible.

Malum in se: wrong in itself.

Malum prohibition: wrong because it is prohibited by the law.

Mora: delay.

Nemo judex in propria causa: no one ought to be a judge in his own cause.

Nomen juris: a word used in a legal context which is accepted as having a recognised technical meaning, *e.g.* heritage or rape.

Omnia praesumuntor rite et solemniter acta esse: all things are presumed to have been done properly and in the usual manner. A briefer version is *omnia rite acta praesumutur*.

Onus probandi: the burden of proving.

Ope exceptionis: by force of exception.

Pendente lite: during the dependence of an action. Sometimes *pendente processu*.

Per incuriam: by negligence, mistake or error.

Prior tempore potior jure: earlier by time, stronger by right. Applicable in many branches of the law.

Pro indiviso: in an undivided manner.

Probabilis causa litigandi: a probable ground of action.

Quantum valeat: whatever value it may have.

Qui facit per alium facit per se: he who does something using another person is taken to have done it himself.

Quid juris?: what is the law?

Quoad ultra: as regards the rest.

Ratio decidendi: the reason of a decision.

Res gesta: the whole circumstance.

Res ipsa loquitor: the thing speaks for itself.

Res judicata: an adjudicated matter. Once a court has decided a point and all appeals have ended, the unsuccessful party should not be able to reopen the issue in other proceedings.

Res nullius: something which belongs to no one.

Socius criminis: an accomplice in the commission of a crime.

Species facti: the particular or peculiar circumstances of the thing done.

Stare decisis: to follow earlier decisions.

Uberrima fides: the utmost good faith.
Ultimas haeres: last heir.
Ultra vires: in excess of the power granted.
Vergens ad inopiam: approaching insolvency.
Volenti non fit injuria: no wrong is done to someone who consents.

APPENDIX TWO

ANALYSIS OF A CASE

Case law represents the law in action. In the application of common law principles or statutory provisions, judges, sheriffs and other tribunals are faced with taking decisions and justifying or explaining what has been done. While case law is often referred to in practice, the complexity of the individual case is such that a very close study or analysis is necessary. This is to enable a proper understanding to be achieved and thus to be sure of citing the cases correctly.

There has in recent years been a dramatic increase in the number and variety of reports of cases, many of the series being highly specialised. However, the analysis of cases follows the same path for all types of report because the style and content while not identical tend to follow a very similar pattern.

Not all cases, of course, need to be analysed but the important ones should be and there are seven headings to be considered in this context. These are set out below and then applied to a reported case.

1. *The parties*. Neither civil actions nor criminal prosecutions appear in court as theoretical exercises or excuse for debate. Someone (a person or a body) has decided to proceed and an analysis should be clear as to who is involved.

2. *The nature of the case*. An analysis of a case requires to have regard to the law involved. There is a scheme of the law and the case ought to be seen in its legal context. The procedural status should be noted. A case of critical importance (critical, that is, to the parties or the development of the law) may be reported on several points as it makes its way through the courts. Finally, within the scheme of the law and at a particular procedural point the broad legal principle must be identified.

3. *The status of the court*. Reference has already been made to the scheme of the law. There is in the Scottish legal system, as in most others, a hierarchy of courts. An analysis of a case ought to have clear regard to the place of the litigation within the hierarchy.

4. *The issue*. What is the central point of a case? The question is often more easily asked than answered because of the complexity mentioned above. Moreover, in, for example, procedural issues the central point may be some rule which requires to be clarified or settled and in doing so in

favour of the defender further action is defeated, thus ensuring that the pursuer does not or cannot proceed further. In short, some cases are tactical so that it is the consequences of the decision rather than the decision itself that is important.

5. *The facts.* Human behaviour may be said to run in patterns but that is too broad a generality. Judges are apt to say that every case turns on its own facts and circumstances. Lawyers arguing a case tend therefore to look at individual facts in order to distinguish cases, that is take a case out of the need to apply an earlier decision. Alternatively, lawyers may seek to show that the cases are identical ("on all fours") so that the earlier precedent is binding.

6. *The result.* What happened? Many cases have earlier stages where moving towards a decision so that the result in each case has to be clearly understood. decisions on procedural or evidential points may affect the ultimate decision on the merits of the case but one has to be clear as to what happened. It must be emphasised in regard to reported cases that a report often covers a procedural or evidential issue. That issue may be of general importance but the ultimate decision on the merits goes unreported

7. *The reasoning.* Why did a court reach a particular decision? This is especially important in cases of the first rank or where an appeal is in contemplation. One needs to know the reasoning behind the decision. this, incidentally, is one of the major criticisms of juries in criminal cases: a jury does not say why a particular decision was reached.

Regina (Majead) v Immigration Appeal Tribunal

1. *The parties.* Mohammed Ali Majead is the claimant. The Immigration Appeal Tribunal in Lonon is the respondant. The Secretary of State for the Home Department (the Home Secretary) is an interested party in the proceedings.

2. *The nature of the case.* Majead sought to appeal against the refusal of a judge to allow him to challenge a decision of the Immigration Appeal Tribunal in London.

3. *The status of the court.* This reported case records a decision of the Court of appeal (Civil Division) for England and Wales.

4. *The issue.* This matter gives rise to decisions being taken in one jurisdiction, Scotland, with appeals against that decision being taken in another jurisdiction, England and Wales.

5. *The facts.* Majead was an asylum seeker of Iraqi nationality who, having arrived first in England, had later been dispersed to Scotland under a government scheme.

6. *The legal process.* Majead lived in Glasgow. He challenged a decision of an immigration adjudication officer in Glasgow. That challenge was taken by way of an application for leave to appeal. The Immigration Appeal Tribunal in London refused leave to appeal. Majead then challenged the decision to refuse leave to appeal. A single judge refused Majead leave to judicially review the decision of the Immigration

Appeal Tribunal. Majead then challenged the decision not to allow judicial review of the decision of the Immigration Appeal Tribunal. Three judges of the civil appeals court refused leave to challenge the decision of the single judge.

7. *The result.* Majead was in error in trying to appeal in England and Wales a decision taken in Scotland.

8. *The reasoning.* The decision of the Appeal Court was given by Lord Justice Brooke, who said that the English court had no jurisdiction to hear an application for judicial review of the decision of the Immigration Appeal Tribunal sitting in London when the initial decision in respect of Majead's appeal was made by an adjudicator sitting in Scotland.

The considerations that arose on an immigration appeal were different from those arising in cases where the question of forum *conveniens* (the most appropriate court) was considered under private law.

Which court should exercise supervision over the decision of an adjudicator in Scotland was not a matter of private convenience but had constitutional consequences.

While there was some residual jurisdiction in the English court that might be exercised in exceptional circumstances, cases of this kind should be decided by the Court of Session in Scotland.

9. *The conclusion.* This case requires immigration lawyers to have regard to their jurisdictions when contemplating advice on appeals. The case is also of interest to constitutional lawyers as a need for the court to recall the basis of the legal relationship between the constituent parts of the United Kingdom.

APPENDIX THREE

TECHNIQUE FOR ANSWERING EXAM QUESTIONS

In many libraries in universities and colleges collections of past papers are kept for reference. It is relatively easy on a brief reading of these papers to see the likely areas of questioning. Rather than simply selecting questions at random and providing answers, it may be more helpful to set out a few general techniques for answering law examination questions.

Many, but of course not all, law students proceed after graduating to enter the legal profession. Answering questions in law examinations can and does in itself provide training for the practice of law, because many problems in practice require questions to be identified and answered.

One important technique for answering questions in law examinations follows from the application of the acronym RISAB where each letter refers to a different activity.

R. It may seem simplistic to say so, but students need to read the question and, where necessary, read it again. It is crucial to answer the question asked and not the question which the student thinks or believes was asked. The pressure of examination often leads to a superficial viewing of the question rather than a close reading. To re-read the question is likely to lead to an understanding of qualifying words that may make the question of a different nature to that first thought.

I. *Identify* the relevant area of law. Many superficial answers fail to locate the subject matter in its proper place. Thus an answer bearing on, for example, *Glasgow Corporation v Central Land Board* (1956) may be seen in the context of *stare decisis*, precedent and, for Scots lawyers, the binding nature of House of Lords precedents from other United Kingdom jurisdictions.

S. *Set* down the general principles. This is a question of balance and relevance but, having identified the area of law, students answering law questions ought to state the general principles governing the point. Many principles may be stated succinctly with reference to cases or statutes and that should be done to locate the subject matter of the question in the scheme of things, and therefore in the proper context.

A. *Answer* the question asked. If the question is not read correctly at the outset the subsequent answer may be correct technically but irrelevant to the question asked. The student ought then to ensure that the answer is directed to the question in the examination paper. In the practice of law, clients and employers expect reasonably to receive from their lawyer solutions to problems, not some sort of solution which is of passing relevance to a broadly connected problem—the same, by analogy, is expected of law students.

B. *Back up* an answer with authority such as a case or a statute. An examiner in a law examination is generally not looking for a superficial answer which reveals a lack of legal technique. That is only to be expected, for in examining the pleading of a lawyer a judge may look for the authorities that support the propositions made by that lawyer.

Examination questions are not selected at random but, on the contrary, are structured by the examiners to test the students' understanding of specific areas of law. Indeed, the key word is likely to be understanding rather than mere knowledge, and an answer ought to be directed more to demonstrating that insight rather than that a few facts have been committed to memory only to be regurgitated a short time later.

Two constraints on the answering of law questions may be mentioned here. First, and understandably the most pressing, is the constraint of time. There is no point in applying the technique described above in one question and in doing so neglecting the remaining questions. In examinations there is always a question of balance in distributing time and effort. Examinations are passed on the total mark and success is most unlikely to be achieved with one flash of brilliance and a number of partially completed answers.

Secondly, the constraint of space means that even in a given time working at maximum efficiency a student can only use up a certain amount of paper and success in law examinations follows from a correct answer rather than a long one. Concise answers stated with general principles and authorities need not take up much paper. It is certain that the examiners will know their subject so that a clear principle, citing properly a case by its general name (*Donoghue v Stevenson*, or *Donoghue*'s case rather than *Donoghue v Stevenson*, 1932 S.C. (H.L.) 31), alerts the examiner to the student's understanding of the problem under examination. A structured question deserves a structured answer.

APPENDIX FOUR

SAMPLE EXAMINATION QUESTION AND ANSWER PLANS

1. "What is an 'Article 177' reference?"

European Community law is usually simply called Community law. That law constitutes a separate legal order from the systems within the individual Member States. Community law exists for the purpose of achieving the aims of the European Union. These aims constitute in essence an even closer union among the people of Europe and to that end the law is directed at ensuring the free movement between Member States of goods, people, capital and services.

The separate legal order includes the European Court of Justice, which may hear enforcement actions brought against Member States which appear not to be fulfilling the obligations imposed by Community law. The European Court of Justice may also hear references under Art.177.

The European Economic Community Treaty was the foundation document of the European Union. Article 177 of that Treaty permits preliminary references to the European Court of Justice from a national court or tribunal. These references arise out of uncertainties or ambiguities in European law and are intended to obtain a ruling. The aim of the reference is to ensure consistent decisions on validity and interpretation throughout the European Union.

In *Garland v British Rail Engineering Ltd* (1982) the House of Lords suggested that there should be a reference where a novel point of law arose, or where there was no constant series of decisions from the European Court of Justice. The High Court of Justiciary made a reference in *Walkingshaw v Marshall* (1992) but declined to do so in *Westwater v Thomson* (1992).

2. "What is the Scottish Law Commission?"

To be effective a law, any law, must be understandable. It must also be capable of application in modern conditions. There is, therefore, an inherent need in all legal systems for change or at least the ability to be able to change.

Judges on occasions can change the law or decide cases in such a way as to indicate to Parliament that the law needs to be reconsidered. Parliament itself can of course legislate with new laws absolutely or new laws that complement existing common law.

There is, however, merit in having law reform and the rationalisation of existing law considered in a more detached and systematic manner. This may be undertaken in anticipation of the need for change rather than under the pressure of immediate demand.

The Law Commissions Act 1965 established two Law Commissions, and s.2 sets up the Scottish Law Commission for the purpose of promoting the reform of the law of Scotland. The Scottish Law Commission consists of a Chairman and not more than four other commissioners appointed by the Secretary of State and the Lord Advocate.

The functions of both Commissions are set out in s.3 of the 1965 Act. It is the duty of each of the Commissioners to take and keep under review all the law with which they are respectively concerned with a view to its systematic development and reform. Generally, the Commissions work to achieve the simplification and modernisation of the law.

3. "What is a *ratio decidendi* and to what extent is it a clear and useful concept?"

There is a need for the law to be certain. With a hierarchy of courts there is a requirement that the application of the law is uniform. When a court or tribunal decides a case one way or the other a written statement of the reasons for that decision must be given. A written opinion ensures that the reasoning of the court or tribunal is set out and that the ultimate decision has been reached on sound or settled legal principles. The decision can then be placed properly within the hierarchy of legal decisions.

The underlying principle of a judicial decision is termed the *ratio decidendi* and it is only that element of the decision which is binding or persuasive on later courts or tribunals, or others lower down the hierarchy. The *ratio decidendi* is broadly the reason or ground on which a judgment rests. It is the conclusion based on the important facts. It is the principle that emerges from a case. Statements not forming part of the *ratio decidendi* are obiter dictum.

It is a useful concept in that the reporting of decisions of courts and tribunals assists in achieving certainty within the law. This is necessary to ensure, for example, that lawyers can give proper advice to their clients. Changing social and economic conditions may render some law useless in modern conditions. The *ratio decidendi* may assist in limiting the extent to which a member of the public is constrained by older cases. Case law shows the law in action. The *ratio decidendi* of cases based on statute indicate the views of courts and tribunals as to how important parts of statutory law are to be understood.

Some important and complex cases result in several decisions or rulings on various disputed points arising from the same case. There may therefore be multiple *rationes* available for application later. Each separate point becomes a binding point later. The concept of *ratio decidendi* is thus a useful means of identifying the precise decision on individual points.

4. "In Court of Session practice: (a) what is the difference between a preliminary plea and a plea on the merits; (b) what is meant by a plea to the relevancy and how does it differ from a plea to the competency; (c) what is the normal procedure by which a plea to the relevancy is disposed of by the court?"

(a) The distinction between fact and law is always important in law. A question of fact concerns the existence in the past or present of some act or event. A question of law, however, concerns the existence or content or applicability of a law in circumstances that are certain. In a debate in a civil case, a preliminary plea is a debate on questions of law and a plea on the merits is a debate on fact. If the parties are in dispute on fact and law both types of plea may be heard.

(b) If the parties are at issue, *i.e.* in dispute, on questions of law or both questions of law and fact, their case is put on the procedure roll for a debate. In a plea to the relevancy one of the parties to the case will argue that written claims of the other party are not sufficient in law to justify his claim. In other words even if what is stated or averred in writing is proved it does not amount in law to enough for the case to succeed. A plea to the competency, however, is an attack on the action as a whole with a claim that, for example, the particular claim cannot be made at all or that the pursuer in the case is not entitled to the remedy sought but to some other remedy.

(c) A plea to the relevancy is normally disposed of by the court at the procedure roll. The important point is that a judge alone disposes of the plea on the basis of the closed record and the argument of the lawyers in the case. There is no jury present at this stage.

INDEX

A coelo usque ad centrum
  meaning, 74
A fortiori
  meaning, 74
A mensa et *thoro*
  meaning, 74
A vinculo matrimonii
  meaning, 74
Absolvitor
  meaning, 73
Accountant in Bankruptcy
  role, 38
Accountant of Court
  role, 38
Acts of Adjournal
  Scottish Parliamentary law, and, 48
Acts of Sederunt
  Scottish Parliamentary law, and,
    47–48
Actus non facit reum
  meaning, 75
Ad factum praestandum
  meaning, 75
Ad vitam aut culpam
  meaning, 75
Adhere
  meaning, 73
Adjust
  civil litigation, and, 56
  meaning, 73
Administrative guidance
  sources of law, and, 13
Advise
  meaning, 73
Advocate
  qualifications, 28
  rights of audience, 35
  role, 29–32
Advocates-depute
  role, 37
Advocation
  common law appeals, and, 68
Aggravation
  meaning, 73
Agnate
  meaning, 73
Aliment
  meaning, 73
Alternative dispute resolution
  generally, 71–72
Answer
  meaning, 73

Appeals
  criminal justice, and
    common law appeals, 67–68
    solemn procedure, 65
    summary procedure, 67
  High Court of Judiciary, and
    solemn procedure, 23–24
    summary procedure, 24–25
  House of Lords, and, 14–15
  sheriff court, and, 60
Appellant
  meaning, 73
Arbiter
  meaning, 73
Assoilize
  meaning, 73
Audi alteram partem
  meaning, 75
Aver
  meaning, 73
Avizandum
  meaning, 73

Bona vacantia
  meaning, 75
Bond
  meaning, 73
Brevitatis causa
  meaning, 75
Byelaws
  Scottish Parliamentary law, and, 47

Case law
  and see Precedent
  analysis, 76–78
  European law, and, 40
Casus improvisus
  meaning, 75
Caution
  meaning, 73
Cite
  meaning, 73
Civil courts
  Court of Exchequer, 19
  Court of Session, 16
  Court of Teinds, 19
  Court of the Lord Lyon, 19
  fatal accident inquiries, 22
  House of Lords, 13–15
  Inner House, 16–17
  Judicial Committee of Privy
    Council, 15–16
  Lands Valuation Appeal Court, 20

Outer House, 17–18
Scottish Land Court, 20
Sheriff court, 18–19
statutory tribunals, 20–22
Civil law systems
sources of law, and, 9
Civil litigation
Court of Session, in
debate, 56–57
introduction, 55–56
jury trial, 58
petitions, 59
proof, 57
reclaiming motions, 58
summary trial, 57–58
diligence, 60
evidence, 60
House of Lords, in, 59
introduction, 53–55
sheriff court, in
appeals, 60
ordinary causes, 59
small claims, 60
summary causes, 59
Closed record
civil litigation, and, 56
Cognate
meaning, 73
Common law appeals
generally, 67–68
Common law systems
sources of law, and, 9
Complaint
summary procedure, and, 66
Conclusion
meaning, 73
Condescendence
civil litigation, and, 55
Constitutional conventions
sources of law, and, 12
Constitutional legislation
UK Parliamentary law, and, 44–45
Contra bones mores
meaning, 75
Council of Ministers
European law, and, 40–41
Council on Tribunals
statutory tribunals, and, 20–21
Court of Exchequer
jurisdiction, and, 19
Court of Session
debate, 56–57
diligence, 60
evidence, 60
introduction, 55–56
jurisdiction, and, 16
jury trial, 58
petitions, 59

proof, 57
reclaiming motions, 58
stare decisis, and, 51–52
summary trial, 57–58
Court of Teinds
jurisdiction, and, 19
Court of the Lord Lyon
jurisdiction, and, 19
Courts and tribunals
civil courts
Court of Exchequer, 19
Court of Session, 16
Court of Teinds, 19
Court of the Lord Lyon, 19
fatal accident inquiries, 22
House of Lords, 13–15
Inner House, 16–17
Judicial Committee of Privy
Council, 15–16
Lands Valuation Appeal Court,
20
Outer House, 17–18
Scottish Land Court, 20
Sheriff court, 18–19
statutory tribunals, 20–22
criminal courts
district court, 26–27
drug courts, 27
High Court of Judiciary, 23–26
House of Lords, 22–23
Judicial Committee of Privy
Council, 23
Sheriff court, 26
introduction, 13
Courts-martial
criminal jurisdiction, and, 22–23
Criminal courts
district court, 26–27
drug courts, 27
High Court of Judiciary
introduction, 23
references to court, 25
solemn procedure, 23–24
summary procedure, 24–25
trials, 25–26
House of Lords, 22–23
Judicial Committee of Privy
Council, 23
Sheriff court, 26
Criminal justice
common law appeals, 67–68
evidence, 68
forum
introduction, 62–63
solemn procedure, 63–65
summary procedure, 66–67
introduction, 61
public prosecution, 61–62

solemn procedure
    appeals, 65
    first appearance, 63–64
    generally, 63
    indictment, 64
    introduction, 62–63
    petition, 63
    trial, 65
summary procedure
    appeals, 67
    complaint, 66
    generally, 66
    intermediate diet, 67
    introduction, 62–63
    trial, 67
Crown agent
    role, 37
Crown Office cicrulars
    administrative guidance, and, 13
Custom
    sources of law, and, 11

Damages
    civil remedies, and, 53
Damnum
    meaning, 73
Damnum injuria datum
    meaning, 75
Debate
    civil litigation, and, 56–57
Declaratory judgments
    civil remedies, and, 53
Decree
    meaning, 73
Defences
    civil litigation, and, 56
Defender
    meaning, 74
Delectus personae
    meaning, 75
Delegata potestas non potest delegari
    meaning, 75
Delegated legislation
    generally, 47–48
Delict
    meaning, 74
Development of Scots law
    eighteenth century, 4–6
    feudal period, 1–2
    introduction, 1
    later middle ages, 2–3
    modern period, 7–8
    nineteenth century, 6–7
    union of the crowns, 3–4
Devolution issues
    civil jurisdiction, and, 15–16
Diligence
    civil litigation, and, 60

Direct effect
    enforcement of European
      legislation, and, 41–42
Directives
    European law, and, 40
Discussion on legal aspects
    civil litigation, and, 56–57
Disputed questions of law/facts
    civil litigation, and, 54–55
District courts
    criminal jurisdiction, and, 26–27
Divorce
    civil remedies, and, 54
Drug courts
    criminal jurisdiction, and, 27

Ejusdem generis
    statutory interpretation, and, 49
European Convention on Human
    Rights
    sources of law, and, 12–13
European Court of Justice
    European law, and, 40
    stare decisis, and, 51
European legislation
    enforcement, 41–42
    generally, 40–41
    UK law, and, 42–43
European Parliament
    European law, and, 41
Evidence
    civil litigation, and, 60
    criminal justice, and, 68
Exam questions
    answering techniques, 78–80
    sample answer plans, 80–82
Expression *uniuus est exclusio alterius*
    statutory interpretation, and, 49
External aids
    statutory interpretation, and, 49
Extract
    meaning, 74

Fatal accident inquiries
    civil jurisdiction, and, 22
Fee
    meaning, 74
Financial legislation
    UK Parliamentary law, and, 44
First appearance
    solemn procedure, and, 63–64
Forum for criminal justice
    introduction, 62–63
    solemn procedure
      appeals, 65
      first appearance, 63–64
      generally, 63
      indictment, 64

introduction, 62–63
petition, 63
trial, 65
summary procedure
appeals, 67
complaint, 66
generally, 66
intermediate diet, 67
introduction, 62–63
trial, 67
Franks Committee
statutory tribunals, and, 20
Future, issues for the
alternative dispute resolution, 71–72
introduction, 68
Public Defender, 70
rights of audience, 70
Scottish Parliament, 68–70

"Golden rule"
statutory interpretation, and, 48
Glossary
introduction, 72–73
Latin maxims and phrases, 74–76
technical terms, 73–74

Hansard
statutory interpretation, and, 49
Hearing of evidence
civil litigation, and, 57
Heritage
meaning, 74
High Court of Judiciary
appellate capacity
solemn procedure, 23–24
summary procedure, 24–25
introduction, 23
references to court, 25
stare decisis, and, 52
trials, 25–26
Highway Code
administrative guidance, and, 13
House of Lords
civil jurisdiction, and, 13–15
civil litigation, and, 59
criminal jurisdiction, and, 22–23
stare decisis, and, 51
Hybrid legislation
UK Parliamentary law, and, 45
Hybrid systems
sources of law, and, 9

Impeachment
civil jurisdiction, and, 13
Indictment
solemn procedure, and, 64

Induciae
civil litigation, and, 55
Inner House
civil jurisdiction, and, 16–17
stare decisis, and, 51–52
Institutional writings
sources of law, and, 10–11
Institutions
development of Scots law, and, 4
Interdict
meaning, 74
Intermediate diet
summary procedure, and, 67
Internal aids
statutory interpretation, and, 49
Interpretation of legislation
generally, 48–49

Judges
role, 35
Judicial Committee of Privy Council
civil jurisdiction, and, 15–16
criminal jurisdiction, and, 23
stare decisis, and, 51
Judicial factor
meaning, 74
Judicial separation
civil remedies, and, 54
Junior counsel
qualifications, 28
rights of audience, 35
role, 29–32
Jurisdiction of courts
civil courts
Court of Exchequer, 19
Court of Session, 16
Court of Teinds, 19
Court of the Lord Lyon, 19
fatal accident inquiries, 22
House of Lords, 13–15
Inner House, 16–17
Judicial Committee of Privy Council, 15–16
Lands Valuation Appeal Court, 20
Outer House, 17–18
Scottish Land Court, 20
Sheriff court, 18–19
statutory tribunals, 20–22
criminal courts
district court, 26–27
drug courts, 27
High Court of Judiciary, 23–26
House of Lords, 22–23
Judicial Committee of Privy Council, 23
Sheriff court, 26
introduction, 13

Jury trial
civil litigation, and, 58
Jus commune
meaning, 74
Jus feudale
development of Scots law, and, 4
Justices of the peace
role, 36

Keeper of the Registers of Scotland
role, 39

Lands Valuation Appeal Court
civil jurisdiction, and, 20
Law agent
and see **Solicitor**
generally, 32
Law Commissions
UK Parliamentary law, and, 45
Law officers
role, 36–37
Legal officials
judges, 35
justices of the peace, 36
sheriffs, 36
stipendiary magistrates, 36
Legislation
delegated, 47–48
European
enforcement, 41–42
generally, 40–41
UK law, and, 42–43
generally, 39–40
interpretation, 48–49
introduction, 9
Scottish Parliamentary
generally, 45–46
stages, 46
UK Parliamentary
introduction, 43
special legislation, 44–45
stages, 43–44
Lex nil furstra facit
meaning, 75
Lex non cogit ad impossibilia
meaning, 75
Liferent
meaning, 74
Literal/liberal approach
statutory interpretation, and, 48
Local legislation
UK Parliamentary law, and, 45
Locus standi
meaning, 74
Lord Advocate's department
role, 37
Lord Treasurer's Remembrancer
role, 38

Malum in se
meaning, 75
Malum prohibition
meaning, 75
Marginal notes
statutory interpretation, and, 49
"Mischief rule"
statutory interpretation, and, 48
Mixed systems
sources of law, and, 9
Mora
meaning, 75

Nemo judex in proprio causa
meaning, 75
Nobile officium
common law appeals, and, 68
Nomen juris
meaning, 75
Noscitur a sociis
statutory interpretation, and, 49
Notary public
meaning, 74
role, 29

Obiter dicta
precedent, and, 50–51
Omnia praesumuntor rite et solemniter acta esse
meaning, 75
Onus probandi
meaning, 75
Ope exceptionis
meaning, 75
Open record
civil litigation, and, 56
Orders in/of Council
Scottish Parliamentary law, and, 47
Ordinary causes
civil litigation, and, 59
Outer House
civil jurisdiction, and, 17–18
stare decisis, and, 52

Parole evidence
meaning, 74
Peerage claims
jurisdiction, and, 14
Pendente lite
meaning, 75
Per incuriam
meaning, 75
Performance
civil remedies, and, 53
Personal injury claims
jury trial, and, 58
Personal legislation
UK Parliamentary law, and, 45

Personnel
  Accountant in Bankruptcy, 38
  Accountant of Court, 38
  advocate
    qualifications, 28
    rights of audience, 35
    role, 29–32
  advocates-depute, 37
  Crown agent, 37
  introduction, 27
  junior counsel
    qualifications, 28
    rights of audience, 35
    role, 29–32
  Keeper of the Registers of Scotland, 39
  law officers, 36–37
  legal officials
    judges, 35
    justices of the peace, 36
    sheriffs, 36
    stipendiary magistrates, 36
  Lord Advocate's department, 37
  Lord Treasurer's Remembrancer, 38
  notaries public, 29
  police, 39
  prison service, 39
  qualifications
    advocate, 28
    notaries public, 29
    solicitor, 28
    solicitor advocate, 29
  Queen's counsel
    qualifications, 28
    rights of audience, 35
    role, 29–32
  Queen's Remembrancer, 38
  Registrar General, 39
  Reporter, 37–38
  rights of audience
    introduction, 33
    lawyers, 35
    non-lawyers, 34
  senior counsel
    qualifications, 28
    rights of audience, 35
    role, 29–32
  solicitor
    qualifications, 28
    rights of audience, 35
    role, 32–33
  solicitor advocate
    qualifications, 29
    rights of audience, 35
  Solicitor to the Secretary of State
    for Scotland, 38
  standing junior counsel, 37

Petitions
  civil litigation, and, 59
  criminal procedure, and, 63
Pleas-in-law
  civil litigation, and, 54
Police
  role, 39
Preamble
  statutory interpretation, and, 49
Precedent
  generally, 49–50
  introduction, 10
  obiter dicta, 50–51
  ratio decidendi, 50
  stare decisis, 51–52
Prerogative legislation
  sources of law, and, 10
Prescription
  meaning, 74
Prevention
  civil remedies, and, 53
Prior tempore potior jure
  meaning, 75
Prison service
  role, 39
Private legislation
  UK Parliamentary law, and, 45
Private member's Bills
  UK Parliamentary law, and, 45
Privileges, breach of
  civil jurisdiction, and, 13
***Pro* indivisio**
  meaning, 75
Probabilis causa litigandi
  meaning, 75
Procurators Fiscal
  fatal accident inquiries, and, 22
Proof
  civil litigation, and, 57
Public defender
  generally, 70
Public prosecution
  criminal justice, and, 61–62
Pursuer
  meaning, 74

Qualifications of legal profession
  advocate, 28
  notaries public, 29
  solicitor, 28
  solicitor advocate, 29
Quantum valeat
  meaning, 75
Queen's counsel
  qualifications, 28
  rights of audience, 35
  role, 29–32

Queen's Remembrancer
role, 38
Qui facit per alium facit per se
meaning, 75
Quid juris
meaning, 75
Quoad ultra
meaning, 75
Quonian Attachiamenta
development of Scots law, and, 3

Ratio decidendi
meaning, 76
precedent, and, 50
Real right
meaning, 74
Reclaim
meaning, 74
motions, 58
Reduction
civil remedies, and, 53
Reform proposals
alternative dispute resolution, 71–
72
introduction, 68
Public Defender, 70
rights of audience, 70
Scottish Parliament, 68–70
Regiam Majestatem
development of Scots law, and, 3
Registrar General
role, 39
Regulations
European law, and, 40
Reparation
meaning, 74
Reporter
role, 37–38
Res gesta
meaning, 76
Res ipsa loquitur
meaning, 76
Res judicata
meaning, 76
Res nullius
meaning, 76
Resile
meaning, 74
Rights of audience
future issues, 70
introduction, 33
lawyers, 35
non-lawyers, 34
Rules
Scottish Parliamentary law, and, 47

Schedules
statutory interpretation, and, 49

Scottish Land Court
civil jurisdiction, and, 20
Scottish Parliament
future changes, 68–70
Scottish Parliamentary legislation
generally, 45–46
stages, 46
Senior counsel
qualifications, 28
rights of audience, 35
role, 29–32
Sheriff court
civil jurisdiction, and, 18–19
civil litigation, and
appeals, 60
ordinary causes, 59
small claims, 60
summary causes, 59
criminal jurisdiction, and, 26
stare decisis, and, 52
Sheriffs
role, 36
Small claims
civil litigation, and, 60
Socius criminis
meaning, 76
Solatium
meaning, 74
Solemn procedure
appeals, 65
first appearance, 63–64
generally, 63
indictment, 64
introduction, 62–63
petition, 63
trial, 65
Solicitor
qualifications, 28
rights of audience, 35
role, 32–33
Solicitor advocate
qualifications, 29
rights of audience, 35
**Solicitor to the Secretary of State for
Scotland**
role, 38
Sources of Scots law
administrative guidance, 13
constitutional conventions, 12
custom, 11
European Convention on Human
Rights, 12–13
formal
introduction, 8–9
minor, 10–11
major, 9–10
informal, 11–13
institutional writings, 10–11

introduction, 8
legislation
    delegated, 47–48
    European, 40–43
    generally, 39–40
    interpretation, 48–49
    introduction, 9
    Scottish Parliamentary, 45–46
    UK Parliamentary, 43–45
precedent
    generally, 49–52
    introduction, 10
    prerogative legislation, 10
    quasi-sources, 11–13
Species facti
    meaning, 76
Specific implement
    meaning, 74
Stages of legislation
    Scottish Parliamentary, 46
    UK Parliamentary, 43–44
Standing junior counsel
    role, 37
Stare decisis
    meaning, 76
    precedent, and, 51–52
Statutory instruments
    Scottish Parliamentary law, and, 47
Statutory tribunals
    civil jurisdiction, and, 20–22
Stipendiary magistrates
    district court, and, 27
    role, 36
Summary causes
    civil litigation, and, 59
Summary decree
    civil litigation, and, 56
Summary procedure
    appeals, 67

complaint, 66
    generally, 66
    intermediate diet, 67
    introduction, 62–63
    trial, 67
Summary trial
    civil litigation, and, 57–58
Summons
    civil litigation, and, 55
Suspension
    common law appeals, and, 67–68
Sustain
    meaning, 74

Title to sue
    meaning, 74
Treaties
    European law, and, 40
Trial
    solemn procedure, and, 65
    summary procedure, and, 67

Uberrima fides
    meaning, 76
UK Parliamentary legislation
    introduction, 43
    special legislation, 44–45
    stages, 43–44
Ultimas haeres
    meaning, 76
Ultra vires
    meaning, 76

Vergens ad inopiam
    meaning, 76
Volenti non fit injuria
    meaning, 76

TITLES IN THE
LAWBASICS SERIES

100 Cases That Every Scots Law
Student Needs to Know
General Editor: Kenneth McK.
Norrie
ISBN: 0414 014 626

Agency *Law*Basics
Aidan ODonnell
ISBN: 0414 012 305

Commercial *Law*Basics, 2nd Ed
Nicholas Grier
ISBN: 0414 015 371

Constitutional *Law*Basics, 2nd Ed
Jane Convery
ISBN: 0414 014 340

Contract *Law*Basics, 2nd Ed
Alasdair Gordon
ISBN: 0414 015 126

Criminal *Law*Basics
Clare Connelly
ISBN: 0414 012 313

Delict *Law*Basics
Gordon Cameron
ISBN: 0414 012 33X

E.C. *Law*Basics
Janet Paterson
ISBN: 0414 014 030

Evidence *Law*Basics
David Sheldon
ISBN: 0414 012 364

Family *Law*Basics
Elaine Sutherland
ISBN: 0414 012 321

Human Rights *Law*Basics
Alastair Brown
ISBN: 0414 013 980

Property *Law*Basics
Ken Swinton
ISBN: 0414 013 735

Succession *Law*Basics
Alasdair Gordon
ISBN: 0414 013 107

Trusts *Law*Basics
Roderick Paisley
ISBN: 0414 013 301

The above titles are all available from your local bookstore.

For further information on titles published by
W. Green, The Scottish Law Publisher, you can visit our website at:

www.wgreen.co.uk